Reflections III
THE MAGIC BEYOND THE PAIN

"THE JOURNEY, MY IMPACT, THEIR IMPACT"

Dalia Vernikovsky

Reflections III The Magic Beyond the Pain
Copyright © 2024 by Dalia Vernikovsky

ISBN: 979-8895311066 (sc)
ISBN: 979-8895311073 (e)

All rights reserved. No part of this publication may be reproduced, distributed, or transmitted in any form or by any means, including photocopying, recording, or other electronic or mechanical methods, without the prior written permission of the publisher and/or the author, except in the case of brief quotations embodied in critical reviews and other noncommercial uses permitted by copyright law.

The views expressed in this book are solely those of the author and do not necessarily reflect the views of the publisher, and the publisher hereby disclaims any responsibility for them.

Writers' Branding
(877) 608–6550
www.writersbranding.com
media@writersbranding.com

Table of Contents

Reflections: The Journey Unfolds 1
    A True Poem–Reflections 2
    Poems 4
    Midnight Poem 5
    Language of the Heart 7

The Painful Moments In Life
    Turmoil or is it? 10
    The World in Pain 11
    Bruised Ties 12
    Yom Kippur 14

Beyond The Pain To Magical Moments
    Time to Write 18
    What to say 19
    Another Chapter 20
    The world as I feel its magic 21
    Different Paths, All the Same 22
    We have the power 24
    Someday Soon 26
    The Spirit Continues to Shine 27
    The flow of life 28
    Chapters to be written 30
    Forever Searching 32
    Forever Young 33
    Glorious Spirit 34
    Journey Back 35
    Life's Passions 36
    Life's Roadmap 37
    My Dreams 39

Daily Life **41**
    Another Fight 42
    The Beach 44
    A Thought 45
    My dedication to tomorrow 47
    Fleeting moments 49
    Another Year 50
    Here and now 52
    Paths 54
    Hope for the Present 55
    Give it meaning 57
    Bridges to Cross 58
    Common Sense is Not Common 62
    Time 63

Phases of Our Lives **64**
    Phases of our lives 66
    Transitioning 68
    Birthdays 70
    Storm, Sun & Rainbows 71
    Forever Searching 73
    What is next 75
    Count the Many 76
    What to say 77
    Today 78
    Chapters to be written 79
    My Dreams Give it meaning 81

Family & Friends & More **83**
    My Son 84
    Mom 86
    Daddy 87
    My Brother Zeev 88

My Sister 89
To My Newfound Family in New York! 90
My Special Neighbors 91
My Close Friend Found... 92
To That Special Friend and my Cat Angel 93
My special Lupe 94
To my special Friend Lori 95
Bond of Friendship 96
Mom's Angel... 97
Friends 98
Angels 99
Tigers & Dragons 100
My Extended Children 102
Family & Friends... 104
Our Special Caretaker–Another Angel 106
My special one 107
Marriage Vows... 108
Friendship Overseas 109
Valentine's Day... 111
World of Trust.. 113
Strange Feelings 115
My Tunte 117
My Adopted Family 119
My special angel Nadia.. 121

My Special Extended Family 123
Nitro.. 124
Sammy My special Princess 126
Mynka, Our Puppy–Cat... 127
Bebe A story of life so fragile... 129
Sheba My Special Quirky One.. 130
Coco That special foster failure.. 132

Reflections 3 ....**135**
    Journey Back (a Musical) 136
    Never Getting Old.. 137
    Perspective 139
    Reaching for Gold 140
    The Future is mine, and to be more......................... 142
    Thoughts... 143
    The flow of life 144
    Who Inspires me?... 146

The Second Half The Understanding **149**
    Reflections 3... 150
    Contentment 151
    Who You Are 153
    A Special Day 154
    Emerging anew... 155
    Moments of Time 157
    Today.. 158
    A Day in the Life 159
    Moments of Time 161
    My wish 162
    Perspective 163
    Change of Course... 164
    Our Paths Unfold 165
    My Life... 166
    My Journey... 167
    Serenity 168
    My eternal optimism 170
    World of Possibilities 171
    Dalia's Strong Self Emerges 172
    Time to Write... 173
    Time is Passing–Emotions strong, lasting 174

Reflections:
The Journey
Unfolds

1st Chapter
A True Poem — Reflections

Life is so precious, so sweet, unpredictable and always tumultuous We are borne with its energies, yet live as though we have forgotten We move through its wonders, blinded, as though in a haze,
As though lost in some trance, lost in a maze Deaf to the birds chirping every day,
So sad that we miss that wonder in any phase.
And even flowers bloom where there is little to sustain, Defiant, showing desire to live, through the good, through the pain,
Life is an oxymoron–leaving us breathless, in love, and hopeless and sad,
We are children always, searching to learn,–learning often without knowing We can be forever young, or old from the day we are born
–neither is our soul pure, neither are we good nor bad We crave attention, yet relish solitude and quiet time
We need to be loved, yet often cannot handle love's overwhelming grasp, We live as though we have forever, when truly, we should cherish every breath, every beat of time.
How often do we say we really will remember?
How often do we drown in 'busy' and feel remorseful as we again, play this word years later?
That is typical, and human, and true to our natures We are creatures that live, and love, and hurt and regret,
We are best when we have learned one lesson, forever set, We are best if our 'good' actually wins over our 'bad'; When we appreciate, and share, and enrich our world.
Whether it is to a someone, or something, or grand charity to that world, We will be so much more, with amazing stories untold,
As we continue to experience the wealth of knowledge and emotion, As we absorb what we have…
And live with passion, and greatness and devotion.

Pass this on to all that care,
What will be remembered, if only for a moment,–'I' and my words to share
Live life complete, forget regrets, learn from the past
It has made you who you are, the individual finally cast.
Our world needs every one of us, every soul devoted to the cause, Once we have finally come to accept who we are, we need to pause. And then use all our power and energy to the happiness in giving, To those who have not learned the absolute wonder of living
Love and Laughter always, Dalia

Poems

A poem is like a song to be sung A torrent of words to be written
Like a canvas awaiting the paint to be flung
It voices the sounds echoed in the crevasses of our mind
Thoughts that flicker and float like so many snowflakes
One of a kind
So much buzzing and loud chit–chat, impossible for one to unwind.
Poems are but one expression of the 'voice' in our souls
Like so many glances through the pathways to our goals,
Can we not capture the essence of the part,
Forever bound to our feelings and heart?
So much spark and fire,
Calm and desire,
Will and spirit, unleashed as turmoil, yet inspire?
Take this energy and feel it gleaning,
Its raw foundation, formed to purpose and meaning,
To a wonderful creation that empowers the soul to find focus and vision
And live the lives full of strength, not indecision,
Here is the song simply expressed and endeared
The words already written, one's life being sung
Every moment sensualized and revered
Life flowing freely, words formulated and strung
Into songs of expressions that have explored, not feared.

Love and Laughter always,
Dalia

Midnight Poem

It is the middle of the night, and all are asleep
Everything is still, quiet, the silence, so very deep,
And in that vast empty time–I should be resting, not be awake,
It seems I am thinking, restless, thoughts I cannot shake,
I forever look for the perfect world, the most sensational feeling,
It should be for everyone, it should be the ultimate healing.
Why cannot I reach to the heavens, to pluck each illuminating star,
Why is it that with such a pure heart, they are still so untouchable, so very far?
I journey each day, grateful for the wonders on my way,
Knowing that I have found the fortunes few seem to find,
In awe of the fact that the beauty of each moment is in the eyes of only those that 'see' it, even the blind.

Yet, my journey seems not to find its path as of yet,
Not that I haven't searched, and done so with no regret..
But elusive it is, as most everyone does know,
It is the same for all, and only differs for those that grow,
And pursue in earnest the magical path of simply giving,
Not concerned or questioning that which may not be understood by the living.
So onward I shall go, and not remorse, and not ponder,
I cannot have each day end in absolute wonder,
It is enough to know that I 'win' more than I 'lose',
I have blessings far beyond most people could ever chose,
And I will find the way, I am certain as is my destiny,
And it will be the one filled with love and harmony.

And if on that way, it will not be as I quite would want or picture,
I will remember that life is as an endless ebb and flow, not a fixture,
And although I may not have reached my goal that day,

I will fight and win and eventually have my way,
The inevitable joy of life is in the magic that is felt in this instant, Search no
more for the truth that is ever so close,
and if we only understood never distant.

Love and Laughter always,
Dalia

Language of the Heart

The poems I write, so freely, so true, so stark
Some are from the depths of places hidden, and dark,
Ultimately, always,–needing expression, a voice
In the path of life,, a way to express my choice,
And always a path to remember the light
To remember how important it is for our spirit, to define, to fight.

Our lives, in constant evolution, amazing, the 'message' we can send, Each day
different, profound, so much to 'see' and feel if we were to tend,
To the needs of ourselves, of our loved ones, of our world,
If we were to just let our intuitions, our minds, our hearts unfold, Yes–I am one
of those fortunate, can express on paper, endowed,–
as I watch my words flow and take shape–something I am less inclined to do aloud.

As the words take shape before they simply vaporize away,
I find the meaning of so many parts of the mystery of each day,
As I continue my journey through the maze of my life,
I will find ways to deal with changing images that still cut like a knife, But am
more focused on new feelings, new joys that caress,
And remind myself, and all who should heed,
that we are here for a short time, and are always blessed.

So few in the world understand the days that fly by, and are gone,
So many miss what is 'there'–the beauty, the dusk and the dawn,
I indeed am endowed with a spirit that questions but knows the why As the
days unfold, and emotions can soar unimaginably high
I do, I dare, I feel each day as it comes and goes,
And help those blind, to see as the world's magic, as it ebbs and flows To those
that do not understand, I say–stop and listen and hear
Each day's miracle is in each tick of the beat of your heart and so clear

That what is the difference in my abundant joy and lift
As I know, to the depth of my core, that what I have now, a gift,
And forever the memory of each day should be truly faced
With the knowledge that it is to be live it, loved and never ever be erased

Love and Laughter always,
Dalia

The Painful Moments In Life

Turmoil or is it?

Here it is another day, and I have failed to conquer all that may concern
I have such high expectations, of myself, when emotions burn,
My nerves sometimes raw from worry and my nerves fray
When I know I can do so much better and I should
end with love, the end of the day,
Here I am with too many thoughts of what I should have done,
When I should be in the midst of offering frolic and fun,

Life is fleeting, that is not a new revelation–nor something new to me,
I know of life that can be twisted, and times I need to flee,
In my mind and in my heart, a soul so light,
In my best, only the desire to bring more love, and less fight,
And yet, in these moments, I am shamefully lacking,
I end up in turmoil, in a mood of 'attacking'
I will work on my powers, my soul ready to learn,
And stop the terrible spiral of emotion and churn,
I am here to bring so much more, so much love and laughter,
I can bring the feeling that follows soon after,
Only the expression of joy and happiness should stay
In the memories we create each and every day

So here I am, one more day passed, good and bad,
I will work to erase the moments of biting and sad,
And replace them with many more of laughter and glee,
So that when I look back, the pictures to see,
I will follow the eyes that return the depth of the love in my soul
And those many special moments to give,–as is my role.

Love and Laughter always,
Dalia

The World in Pain

The paper comes every day bearing the news,
Full of calamity, and tragedy and stories that rarely bemuse,
Stories of pain and suffering, and poverty and sin,
Stories of rage and war and disputes that inevitably no one can win, Tales of
woe and sorrow that assault so much of our minds,
Yet we continue each day as though it did not happen, one finds.

Why is that, you ask? Does no one really care?
Can we be so crass as to not want to see what we cannot bear?
Or is it that there is so much of it, and it almost seems routine,
So much of it that we lose perspective, and our senses become less keen, We
have our lives, and then the lives of those we love and cherish,
And then there is mankind, and lives,–how can we stop those that perish?

So my friends, and all that may read these words of reflection and desire,

I know that no matter, we have more will and more fire,
We have what it takes to make a difference, if we just pause,
We have what it takes to help so many that need, at least one cause,
And then each one has added a drop closer to that rarity,
Of incredible humanness and in–born charity.

That, my friends is what I write to you today,
To read the paper each day, and walk not so quickly away,
Our lives are busy, but the large picture leaves little behind of importance,
What will be etched as a part of us is how we lived, if there was substance,
The true reflection will be what we have done so the news may someday be
written in hews of happiness and gold,
The true day to come as the paper fills our heart with happiness as all the
wonderful stories unfold ..

Love and Laughter always,
Dalia

Bruised Ties

The depth of my heart rages with emotion
Overwhelming feeling that I may have failed, in spite of my deep sense of devotion,
To both my own family, who I promised to cherish and watch,
And to the concept of it, as I have always wanted and loved so much.
The family–moms and dads and sons and daughters,
The core of it all, with an importance as significant as foods and waters.

An extension of ourselves, in our children and theirs too,
It has always been so, the most important–the glue.
So with deepest of feelings and guilt, no matter why,
I parted ways and broke the bond, and let myself cry,
But from all that was hurt, and all that seemed bad,
There are parts that aren't necessarily forlorn or sad,

I have embraced the extension of my ex, now my friend, my dear,
His family and prior ones, whether afar or near,
So I am blessed to have gained that part and impart on my son to protect,
His many family and friends whose lives he will affect,
And embrace the concept, his character strong and vibrant
To himself and who he meets,
A testimony that the concept indeed lives anew and the odds it beats,

I, as most, must patch my life back together, as best I know how,
As we learn more about ourselves, the most important is 'now',.
We need to revel in the time given us anti revere those that we cherish,
Indeed, life is meaningless without experiencing love before we perish, The discovery of that fact enriches the paths we chose,
And ~empowers us to think as winners no matter what we do, and never lose.

I am one of those fortunate ones, to have discovered my way,
There is much more to appreciate' in each and every day.
But my love for friends and family has intensified in magnitudes as well.

Although I have not had enough time to really contemplate and dwell, On
the profound meaning of all this represents,
I chose to simply live through the precious feeling of such events..
Do this for yourself and all those you can influence on the way,
The family, the core is the driving force that keeps all from going astray,
The love of each other, and the need to connect: to those who care,
As we move through our world, and realize all the wonders yet to share…

That is it–everyone must learn to understand,
The fulfillment, the burning desire to find ourselves, to be complete, That
will come with each one of us–touching a soul, touching a heart, touching
each other,–and generating a strength nothing
on this earth can defeat.
Take good care of yourself, and keep your spirit pure and alive ..
And do what your heart says to you, every moment,
whispering the truth and drive,
And remember, you do not hear it, unless .. you listen, to the beat, to the
force inside, to all that has led us, and guides us to thrive.
Be all that you can be, and continue the journey to be the best. and love this
live, and all it means, every moment,
every breath of every splendid day,
Experience its riches, its pain, its unabashed joy,–in every
sensational, free–spirited way!.

Love and Laughter always,
Dalia

Yom Kippur

Another year has quietly come and gone, awaiting one to be born,
This day of reflection can often lead us silent and forlorn,
As we look at what we have done, and all what we have not,
My expectations always high, the feelings in my gut,
Always wanting to have achieved, to have done so much more,
Always trying to make things right, to mend what I think I tore…

So I look to the heavens, to my Lord, to my inspiration,
Knowing deep down that I am quite human, sometimes filled with strife and hesitation.
Yet, the new day, another chance to leave my mark, to revere in life so grand
Another day to explore the world, every crevasse of this great land,
To act like a bold brush and paint with every color of the rainbow,
To travel and prance, or meander, like the streams that gently flow.

Why not try, Why weep and cry?
This day should not be the 'mourning', but the reflection–the beginning, It should bring resolution of what we can be, of the magic, of our 'winning',
After pondering and reviewing all that has led us to be who we are,
Experience, my friend, is the precious teacher that carves our way, our star.

Never to be erased, often not to be understood,
We cannot allow ourselves to be tortured by memories often to be forgotten, if we just could.
Each story living in a part of our thoughts or dreams,
Often etched in our hearts, and stored forever, it seems…
The better ones always to be brought to our attention,
The bad ones should teach the lessons–that. is their intention…

So as I pray to start this year anew with thoughts so pure,
Yet reminisce on past experiences filled with excitement and allure,
I reflect on all the things I still do not have complete,
And know I would want my imperfections yet to beat,

And spend the day in prayers and void of any other needs,
This cleansing of the soul important to rid the doubts and concentrate on good deeds,

And so the year is fresh, my mind abounds with songs to be sung,
And I move with the rhythm of one feeling yet so young…
I will beat the 'bad' guys, the wrongs of this world,
Who says we can't, we are the hero's of the stories as they unfold!
Each one of us borne with an incredible talent and gift,
Each one of us creating wonderful moments that always uplift.
All the world in turmoil, yet if I look very close,
The true magic and harmony is silently happening, never verbose,

The day-to-day clutter, the day-to-day hum,
The beginning. of a new year, a chance to stretch each part, once numb, And stand tall in the wonders of life so precious,
And otter help in joy, that alone–so infectious,
As to make the deterrence to something, to someone,
And live each day living our best, improving, until our work, our life, is done.

Love and Laughter always,
Dalia

Beyond the Pain To Magical Moments

Time to Write

It is time to write as I enter this New Year,
It is time to write my desire to meet life head on,–leave behind my fear
I am ready, I do believe, for the life yet ahead,
I am so full of anticipation, of this chapter to be read
I look to the heavens,–and to my core as well,
As I know that I have journeyed long,–of course, that is impossible on me to tell!
My life rich with experience, so good and so bad,
I have once yearned for death, unimaginable,–and sad,
That I,–that someone, could reach lows so low to make that call,
And so out of control, that it was easier to fall,
Prey to the worst, and to the thought of such madness
Prey to our mind's own fears, our own sadness,

But here I am, amazingly mighty and strong
Here I am–the gal that survived, with so much more right than wrong Here
I am writing the world of my will, of my power
Here I am as tall as I can tower,
As I proudly move forward to etch these words into your heart,

I am certain that so many of us are all a part,
Of a higher energy, a power to explore and thrill
I am living life with joy, and wonder–and free will.

Next steps–watch out.. as this lady continues to evolve
Watch out, world,–as I deepen my resolve
To make this world a better place,
And find a way to brighten someone's face
As many as possible, as far as I can reach
Happiness and joy and smiles–that, and more, I will teach…

Love and Laughter always,
Dalia

What to say

It is the New Year, a time to renew
I am in the skies again, flying home one more time,
Bone tired, with little energy, and words so few,
And the knowledge that I am not getting younger, definitely in my prime.
What to show for it? What have I done?

Working on so many things to accomplish, but trying with that, to have fun,
Hard to do when there is no time, and deadlines abound,
Hard to reflect when the work never stops, and rest is a desire so profound,
So, as I indeed have time to reflect on a life full of strife and in conclusions,
It also suggests that there is more to do, and to each of us, our own illusions,
To roam, to romp, to look for ways to live without constraints
To find solace in knowing that we are not alone in that space, that magic
that life so often paints

I have searched for so many years to find exactly what?
When I know that it is the everyday that is the magic in itself,
It is that very point we all so often miss until the end.
And often struggle to really feel when turmoil attends
That space is ours, we can chose not to let those feelings guide our decisions,
And forever nurture the core of our being,
To capture the many magical moments of
splendor–to fulfill the true breath of our visions.

Love and Laughter always,
Dalia

Another Chapter

Another season goes by–fall brought bitter cold, leaves that shrivel and die,
But the spirit senses a step into spring,–new foliage,
movement of leaves that whisper and sigh,
In the warming winds of the season, and the excitement of new things emerging,
The plants that have slept, begin slowly peeping through the ground,
What magical beauty and newness in each one, envisioned and found

We are so blessed with the smells and sights that surround us,
But so immersed in our world that we live without notice of what is around us,
Every day should be treasured, and revered,
Instead of the toil and anguish of our world, so feared Every day–a joy–a gift,
Every day–a love of something special that should, our spirits lift

The countless seconds, moments, hours, days and years lost,
To the futility of searching for cold things that can be tossed,
We do not notice what are eyes can see, what our ears can hear,
What our noses can smell, what are senses can 'peer'
What feelings are we to feel from this thing called our heart?
What emotions to be gleaned if we noticed from the start?
So in the latest chapter of my time on this earth as I,
A promise to notice, to absorb, to defy,
The urge to miss those wonders of all that surrounds me,

And immerse myself in my passions and be
That wonder, that glorious part of these surroundings–the spark
For the magical moments that bring our spirits to the light from the dark,
Always, always see the best of what you are, you must
You know in your heart that you do so much good, you are just
So that is what should be with you every day, in every way,
Be that inspiration you are, and that vision, that feeling, never stray.

Love and Laughter always,
Dalia

The world as I feel its magic

As I move into a different life, one that can be one to share,
I need to let my feelings lead and trust–if I dare,
My heart pounds strong, yet cannot still shake all the pain,
I have lived in darkness, and in moments of utter disdain,
I have overcome so very much, yet still ripped by the depth of fear,
Of that cold, the darkness that only my mind can calm, can steer,
Away from those dark places, and into the warm of the light,
Into the areas where I can blossom, I can feel well, and bright,
I can love and I can give, and nothing less but real,
I can believe that someday, will be serenity, and surreal.

Life is so beautiful–only a few in the world actually do truly see,
In the day to day world, there is so much to touch, to feel, to be,
And the blessings that, if touched by the angel above,
Will allow us to live strong, to know our purpose, and always, to love
Those that are our friends, our family, and everything alive and real
Should be the ultimate part of our path, of our feel,
For life takes us on multiple paths and those we touch
And too often do not realize how we need them so much
Ah, dear world, dear time, dear angels, are you listening?
As I watch outside my window–the stars glistening?

Yes, it is ours to live, it is ours to enjoy,
It is our lives to make, to build, to give, to toy,
It is ours to live with ultimate abandon, and ultimate creation,
It can only be our souls that will finally reach that sensation,
When we have fulfilled a special place in our heart, our soul,
And realize that serenity achieved, we are no longer 'apart'–the ultimate goal.

Love and Laughter always,
Dalia

Different Paths, All the Same

Why is it that we are challenged in so many ways?
Look around, and you will find, all of us in our own, gone astray,
Is it that we all have our own battles of demons versus good?,
Astounding raw energy and force in constant turmoil as we decide what we should?

We live, but, are we living,, each moment, the breath of every true tick of time,
So many moments,–how many can we remember, as our lives reach prime.
Who knows,–will we ever, and should we,
As we reach our final resting place, have we found peace,
have we been all we could be?

Through life, we yearn for company and yet remain alone,
within our own world,
It is that we fervently look to do something good,
to unleash a spirit, like a flag unfurled.
Is it God to help our way,–not leave us abandoned as we turn to dust?

I, but a flicker of light in a world full of fascinating hews and colors,
I, but a small voice reaching out knowing I am more,
I am the strength, the power, the enabler of so much good,
I can do anything, a creator, and I will,–as I should
Be a mentor, and a leader and rattle,–make a difference
As I am not going to let my life, my light be for naught,
As I pass from this world into another, I will leave much to be taught.

I WILL be heard, and will have left a mark,
I WILL have created some light in the dark,
And the generations to follow will be enriched
So that each one of me can be the beam so bright, seemingly bewitched
And a deeper flame of so much more of me
That legacy, left, as I find myself in a new world, a new energy…

That is it–everyone must learn to understand,
The fulfillment, the burning desire to find ourselves, to be complete,
That will come with each one of us–touching a soul, touching a heart,
touching each other,–and generating what can not be lost, even apart.
Take good care of yourself, and keep your spirit pure and alive..

And do what your heart says to you, every moment,
whispering the truth and drive,,
And remember, you do not hear it, unless ..you listen, to the beat,
to the force inside, to all that has led us, and guides us to thrive.
Be all that you can be,,, and continue the journey to be the best..
and love this live, and all it means, every moment,
every breath of every splendid day,
Experience its riches, its pain, its unabashed joy,
–in every sensational, free–spirited way!.

Love and Laughter always,
Dalia

We have the power

Rich and powerful, life pulses through our body and soul,
Each day testimony to the miracles, as our stories unfold,
Not creatures, as others of this world, our planet made home,
Different, we learned, as we conquered and captured all that used
To freely roam,
Aggressively pursuing our right to live and multiply,
And establish a heritage for our offspring to grow, when we finally Die.

This has been the way since the beginning, since inception,
With only the strong winning, and colonies multiplying through
Conception, And our kingdom only plagued by others like us that seek,
To control and rule, and master the weak.
The way of the creatures etched deep in our brains,
Mother nature protecting the survival of the race as each Generation wanes.

But as we grow, and as we mature,
There is something else that becomes important and becomes the Allure,
It is more than the passion of survival, of a material need,
It is our spirit that calls deep inside us, and begs to heed,
Questioning and tumultuous, not letting us rest or ignore,
Searching through time yearning to understand what is elusive,
What is it that is 'more'?

Our powers within, our life something beyond the body we Posses,
Our riches measured in understanding the work of compassion, so taxed under duress,
We are the creators of the world that mankind now share
We are unwilling masters of the troubles, of all those that do not
Care,
We must learn to harness the strength endowed in all our Generations,
Given as a gift to our ancestors and to our children of all races, of All nations.
There will be a time that we will realize the depth of this power,
And the intensity of such energy, the likes from which we now Cower,

Our brains not ready for the burden or the vision,
That could unleash us from the cruelty of so much of our
Indecision,
And launch is into a new era, a new generation of good,
As we realize the importance of compassion and giving,
as Important as our need for food.
And prevent new tyranny, wrongs and oppression,
With those that have control as a requisite, a main obsession,
Introducing the 'light' as a way to seek peace and devotion,
For all those around us, who have responded with raw emotion,
And walk the path that were destined to find,
And salvage the future for all our children–and for all of mankind.

Believe it, embrace it, help foster the time to be 'now'!
Whatever the hardships, whatever the price, there will be a vision
To show us 'how',
It has never been the easy path to follow, to chose,
But it will be the difference between what we win or lose,
It will be the legacy left to our children to mold and create,
And the world will be all that we want, and all that we believe, is fate.

Love and Laughter always,
Dalia

Someday Soon

Someday soon I will walk on the beach and hear the whispers of the sand,
Someday soon I will smell the freshness of the waves,
maybe with someone by my side, hand-in-hand, Someday
I will wallow in abundant time, be awash in all I desire,
Indeed, all my growth and determination and fire,
It is not impossible to dream that the time has come, and my dues paid,
That my Karma has been blessed, as I for years, deeply prayed.

My life, as most–a winding road of trial and error, laughter and pain,
It is the path everyone takes in degrees–some of us towards the heavens,
some that will end in vain,
But my path, as is everyone's is unique and special and on a quest,
Mine, as those that strive, is a path where I ultimately must be the best.

The best of my being of my accomplishments–whatever they may be,
A tribute to whatever spirit I finally recognized to be my own,
And the spirit that rose from a life that was blurry since the day I was borne,
NO more–no, not indeed,
For this creature of passion and spirit and destiny lives,–it was freed!

So today I look at my someday…and know it will not be long,
I have been blessed with much family and friends,–and I BELONG,
And with that,–the strength and courage to make my dreams come true.
Because at the end of our days, those that realize what is important, are too few.

My someday is already here.. THAT is my message to all those that wait.
Live life every single second,–that is our fate..
And enjoy every morsel, smell, taste possible–,that someday is–, today.
We cannot live for that tomorrow.. that someday,
It may never come, it was never meant to be God's way,
What is promised–the beauty, sensations, the taste of every minute of time,
The love, the deepest breath, the wildest passion, and every musical chime,
MUST be felt now, in the moment, and savored so very much,
TODAY is the world,–for tomorrow, the angel, our soul, may touch.

Love and Laughter always, Dalia

The Spirit Continues to Shine

There are few people in this world, untouched,
By memories, by deeds, by sights and sounds,
We search for who we are, too often rushed,
To miss the wonders of the world and its beauty,
As we grow and sort through our ways
Astounding images and views and all that is precious amaze,
I have been touched by several souls,
At times in my life that were painful and my spirit lost,
Unable to think that nothing could reach me or console,

So is it that my special friends reached out to my heart,
And would not relent, and set themselves apart,
From the world of hurt and grief, and loneliness,
And offered their unwavering love, their special solace,
And softened the world, and also helped me see
That the world has had heroes galore,
The Anna Frank's whose mark would effect eternity,
And taught me that I, too, must reach for more.

So, to my special ones, I send my love and adoration,
My hopes and my dreams evolve as I strive to leave MY mark,
But your place is secure in my heart and all my admiration,
For all those that believed in me, who reached into the dark,
And taught the child to smile and laugh and shine
And sing and prance and love life out loud!
And whom I consider as a soul, as mine.
Knowing that I, too, will make a difference and make her proud.

The ultimate dreams I know, achieved
And my special ones, forever with me, as they always believed.

Love and Laughter always,
Dalia

The flow of life

We are on an endless journey with no true start or true finish,
Being borne to travel to the end, to die, does not diminish,
What is actually a continuation of experiences by which we grow
Of so many lives to bear, yet explore, in an endless spiritual flow..

Thus what paths we chose all have a reason and magical rhyme,
Never to be understood in the dimension or the limitations of time,
It is a sojourn of endless ecstasy and terrible, lonely tragedy,
Manifested in great joy and paradoxical, unthinkable calamity,

Are we lost through this maze, this sea of time and space?
Is there a spiritual state that must be reached,–is that truly the case?
So many questions we could ask, if we stop to ponder,
Yet we explore each day we are on this earth to wander..
And most of us find no solace or magical answers that heal,
Most of the crowd do not find the paths to strengthen or appeal,
To the important part of their spirit and soul,
The reason for living and what often takes its toll,

Questions, questions.. Does it really matter what it could mean?
When you look around, what is left, what can we glean?
Some of us trek on an endless journey to nowhere,
Those people seemingly live without a doubt or care,
Others spend all their time searching for what, or why

In reverence of something, lost or found, .. oh my, oh my…
In truth and in honesty, in blatant disregard of the fears,
Life has no meaning if we cannot love so deep as to bring us to tears,
Whether it be someone, or something, a friend, lover or object, Whether it
be physical, mental or spiritual manifestation as the subject,
It must be deep, it must be true..
Colors of the rainbow in all their glory and hue…

So passes our lives,, the time ticks away,,
We endure hardships and pain, only to realize the way..
For if we are to truly understand the depth of our feeling,
We must have learned to understand the intensity of the healing,
That comes with empathy and compassion and care,
Forever to repeat in endless lessons that started in despair..

But those that endure, and heal and grow,
For those that understand the world, and God's ebb and flow,
The reward is the richening of everything that is important to feel,
Inexplicable and illumines,–unique with the intensity of something so real.
Sad, isn't it.. that we must suffer to understand what is life..
What is beautiful, what is important begins with so much strife.

Listen! ..Listen, I say.. as I say this with all my heart..
Do not search outside, do not become lost, or try to finish from the start.
Our lives are meant to be filled with so many tests of who we are..
We must trust ourselves, and the voice inside never far..
And enjoy each day.. experience as children in God's paradise…
Enjoy each pain and blessing alike.. take my advise..

Sojourn in peace.. and in simplicity and deep emotion
Forever your way, your travels with love and devotion..
And the road light and filled with incredible sensation
And that all that we are and will be–parts of creation..

Love and Laughter always,
Dalia

Chapters to be written

My mind churns, endlessly processing 'data' from this body and soul
It never rests,–never ceases to work,–that is its role,
The it–the I–a constant question, as all our minds work the same–or do they,
We are souls,–not robots that as we act and ponder–living individual creations,
Amazing more, the years that pass, as we live more, and learn more
We sift through this mind, for answers, for help–to find our core,
We live experiences, good ones, and horrible ones–and yet live on
Are we then smarter, brighter, wiser, happier, content?

Is there a formula, some way, that someone may someday invent?
All of us on these paths,–all will end in the energy we become,
It would be so much easier,–as we sometimes vanish in numb,
Easier to 'disappear' than deal with oneself, or the hurt,
Knowing it is you, the individual, the mind being overt
And then, the other side–of running and hiding,–buzzing and busy
As we cannot find the 'self' at peace if we stopped being dizzy
No answers today, but the stories of all of us are not even yet told,
We must look at all we have done, good deeds and bad, and not fold,
We must strengthen our powers to understand that mind–and where we are,

As we are like books being written, the author–the editor,–the star
We have the gift of life, mostly forgotten in the day to day,
We must stop, and look, and feel and touch,–through the fray,
And imagine for a moment,–each day–how life's beauty, and friends, and family convey
The love in our hearts, and the mind's fear allay
We are writing pages each day we live,–the way we act, the way we feel,
We should count our blessings, and laugh and smile –it IS a big deal
We are our own masters of attitude, of happiness and joy,
We are also those that can make those less fortunate be able to enjoy

By sharing what may–material, or wealth or time or poems,

As we do, you will see that our minds slow the churn, and the mutter,
As we find our way to more serenity of who we are, and rid the clutter
So indeed–write, on paper or in that power of the mind,
And decide only to focus on the good parts–and you will find
The chapters become more beautiful, more real,
And the world that surrounds you, surreal.

Love and Laughter always,
Dalia

Forever Searching

Here again, like so many times before
Traveling on this airplane, people and mayhem galore!
All talkative or reflective, looking out the window at the past
Worlds apart so many strangers going home at last
We so often forget to focus or care
That our lives are passing, it seems so unfair
But there is always a reason that we go where we must
As we grow and mature, we learn to listen and trust
Our internal guide–our feelings and hearts
As God has provided so much of our 'smarts'

So feel strong and confident in all that you do
As life has meaning as long as we live and are true
To what we believe is our mission and core
As our spirits grow and radiate forever more.

That is it–everyone must learn to understand,
The fulfillment, the burning desire to find ourselves, to be complete,
That will come with each one of us–touching a soul, touching a heart,
touching each other,–and generating a strength nothing on this earth can defeat.
Take good care of yourself, and keep your spirit pure and alive..
And do what your heart says to you, every moment, whispering the truth and drive,,
And remember, you do not hear it, unless ..you listen, to the beat, to the force inside,
to all that has led us, and guides us to thrive.
Be all that you can be,,, and continue the journey to be the best.. and love this live, and all it means, every moment, every breath of every splendid day,
Experience its riches, its pain, its unabashed joy,–in every sensational, free- spirited way!

Love and Laughter always,
Dalia

Forever Young

It seems such a short time that I have lived, yet I sense that I am at the prime of my journey.
Not yet having reached my goals, for they are many; not ready to concede it is time to ascend to another place
I have reached a state of mental awareness that betrays my own frustration– not having 'gotten there sooner'
It is hard to imagine that I have so much to offer, and so damn smart that I could not have reached this state –that is the case,
I love life as few people do, with appreciation and sensations that so many miss in the everyday hustle,
I reach for the stars, and am driven to accomplish so much, more than I probably will achieve but so much more than others strive to try,
So I continue my path and struggle to find ways to slow so much of my hustle,
I continue to work, and work, and work, but know that my time will evolve into something new, something unique,
something that will bring happiness, and peace before I die.
How much I cherish these many moments!
They fulfill my soul through the love I feel–the closeness to my son, and my family, and friends
How much I look to so many more of these days, as I long to be that more, and find what happens when this part of my journey ends
NO.. not in death, but as one chapter closes and another unfolds,
Not that I have regretted EVERYTHING, but some–yes,, and in prayer that there is no more,

It seems I have strengthened, as we all must, when we have fallen; yet achieve success in overcoming the worse,
–and somehow live on as never before.
Yes, happiness in indeed within,–a lifetime event that evolves only from one's own self–worth and awareness.
Yes–we all have that ability, that need, the desire,–the responsibility.
Only we have the chance to find our ways, frolic in love and energy as though profoundly moments in carelessness

Love and Laughter always, Dalia

Glorious Spirit

I reach to the stars and float in the warmth of a spiritual sea
Feeling that I can do anything and everything possible–that life
Offers everything needed to be all that I can be!
That all one's growth, in good as well as bad
When sometimes one thinks we are on the verge of going mad!
As we sojourn through moods of passive, happy and sad
All these feelings and more a sour journey leads us stronger, wiser, surer In search of ourselves, our meaning and ultimate destiny
Where our futures are clear and our souls aglow with Harmony!
The lessons to be learned as we wake up every day to the glow of the sun and the smell of the air
Is that gratitude and love is all that we share
And the deeper the understanding and the more intense we live The more we realize that all we have to give
Is love, and thoughts and prayers that show we care,
And that dreams will come true, and blessed the feeling for those that dare.
Love and Laughter always, Dalia

Journey Back

There are so many of us, as I, that grew up in the dark,
In the shadows; cold and pain leaving its mark;
The world was impossible, Anger, hurt, fear, unstoppable,
How can you see when there is no light?
When all you ever do is cower, broken, darkness and night.

Come on, girl, run for your life into the light!
Let's see what what's inside,–that incredible fight!
Fight so the world cannot defeat you!
Might, so that the world cannot beat you!
Fight. To come out of the dark,
This time,,–YOU are the one that is leaving your mark..

Fight.. so the world cannot defeat you,
Might.. so the world cannot beat you,
Out of the dark.. fighting..leaving your mark

Now, world, MY fight, my might,
And into the light.. as is my right!
And guide others to that destiny,–shining so bright!.
Fight, so the world cannot defeat you,
Might, so the world cannot beat you,
Out of the dark, bold, strong;–to always be the light!!

Love and Laughter always,
Dalia

Life's Passions

We live to reach for our dreams,
And ride the ever changing tide of life's streams,
We live, grow, hurt, survive, and live once more,
Our dreams often bashed, and our spirits hurting to the core,

Not I, dear God, no way can my spirit die!
I have lived and survived, and all the odds defy!
No way, I say, can I live another day,
With an empty soul, and my dreams fallen away,

No way, as my passion burns, my spirit yearns,
Yes, my passion strong, and knowing I belong,
To the world of the blessed,
Not of the devil possessed,
Gone are my doubts, my grief and hurt,
Gone are those demons that with my mind flirt,
I am back, with all the heat of desire,

I have yearned for that strength, internal fire..
Not I, no way, as my passion burns, and my spirit strong,
As I realize, I live and I know I belong.
My soul in love with life, with each moment, each day
With energy blessed, and a desire to give in everyway,
Life is a blessing that many do not know
And maybe I can change with a smile, a glow.
Love and Laughter always

Love and Laughter always, Dalia

Life's Roadmap

We were borne with hazy eyes, legs wobbly and weak,
Our focus to grow and walk and speak,
We wrestle with each other, with anyone in our path,
Explore our world, play, frolic make noise, and laugh.
Our minds, simple, uncluttered, riding life's ebb and flow
Our laughter, unabated, tears free as we sense highs and lows,
We are simple and open, feeling and touching,–unbridled
The early journey, before we grow and forget simplicity, entitled.

Yes we are borne with hazy eyes and wobbly feet,
Then blossom, and expand our world,
Feelings now awake, as if a flag unfurled,
Our minds begin to question, why, the good, the bad,
Our minds and hearts begin to question, feelings boil,
Hormones rage, havoc in our veins, and turmoil,
Our spirit wrought with what we can, should, may, may not do.
Interactions become more intertwined and unclear,
Boys and girls suddenly stutter and stammer,
Physical touch, forbidden, confusion and fear.

A world full of grief and waste lay in our paths
Life continues, our journeys each one unique and amazing,
To live and love, but also feel pain and despair
We have parents and friends and loved ones, always love to repair
We look around and must decide which to chose,
It will be the difference in our souls to win or lose.
Yes, we were borne with hazy eyes and wobbly feet,
We have grown and learned the lessons of victory and defeat,
We are here for a purpose, each one must learn and decide,
Whether in songs, or in school, or on ice to glide

Or a professor, a father or mother to impart so much knowledge, Life's
many lessons cannot be taught in college.
Yes, we are borne with hazy eyes and wobbly feet,
Forever learning–our spirits abound with sight and strength as our hearts
beat And that life is more that what we can touch and see,
It is full of magical moments, if our spirits are open to feel
And yes another magical birth of a soul to heal.

Love and Laughter always, Dalia

My Dreams

Life is such a wondrous event full of sorrow and pleasure,
An oxymoron of feelings that cut deep beyond measure.
A torrential storm that can sweep away the very meek,
A motley mixture of sensational happiness, and devastating lows so bleak,
As to bring the strongest of mankind to their knees so weak.

Why is it our destinies to learn our paths through suffering and pain?
Why cannot the way be spewed with flowers and sugar cane?
Will the lessons not be taught, will our minds not ruminate?
Will every day not be a myriad of thoughts to contemplate,
Every path to chose, every decision to review,
Every life one lives touches all the others, as though on cue.

So it is with all the pleasures and the pain I am learning to mark,
Teaching my mind to focus on the dream I wish to ignite and spark,
To the future of the many that await my decision to do..
What has been my desire for oh so many years, not few
And count on my strength to overcome my indecision and disarray
Knowing full well that I am capable of achieving it–today.

My dream, my hopes, my unbound energy to cultivate and give,
Choices we all make can affect how we live..
My chose is my strength, my happiness, my glory,
It is the path I will walk, it is the chapter of my story,
As I walk into the second half of my time since my birth,
The greatest of deeds must be done while still on this earth.

Take heart, my friends and all those that share my fate,
Take notice as I take charge of my life and march to create
The image I project so many times over in my mind,
Of a place no one has, a place full of laughter and acts of kind,
A place I will call home, and surrender all my worries and fears
And rejoice in the magic of many more moments to wipe away all those tears

Love and Laughter always, Dalia

DAILY LIFE

Another Fight

So for another flight through the air
Leaving behind family and friends, those that care,–
Many magical moments slowly dimming, with each passing pebble of time,
Life is fragile,–not to be understood, if we even could,
In the air there is time, an abundance to reflect
Life is a gift, unending swirl of life and events that we often reject
We are, each one, fascinating journeys–tumultuous poetry that never rhyme.

And so I meet a stranger, who has deep eyes that glimmer from his spark
He preaches tale of returning souls, endless lives shining from the dark,
He is a mystic, a scholar,–a friend, a 'seer'
A follower of our destinies–a 'believer'
One who is truly connected with himself, and what he must do,
He is rare among the most,–and there are so few.
I am to be giddy, and free, and reminded how deep is my soul,
I am a 'warrior' he says,–vibrant, energetic, in a specific role,
My karma resonating with so much passion and care
How far I can grow, my mind does not dare,
But I must focus and find my way, dear Lord,
I am intense, and cannot be deterred, as failure I cannot afford,
Will it be through poetry,–I wish it could be,
As I write with so much passion, easy to see So once again,
I search for that elusive answer,
That can only come from within, from what I know, once a dancer,
I love to swirl, to feel, to touch,

I am so full of energy, I crave to love so very much,
Okay I know–it is indeed, inside of me,
That love, that mystery, that mischievous, that glee
That amazing part of all of us given time on earth,
Yet most, and me, have not claimed it from birth.

So dear Lord, and all that is precious and true
Yes I know, my angels are here too,–to guide me to do
Hurry, please, dear ones, I am so late in the game,
I have so much to do once I will claim,
My rightful place in this time, in this unique and special space,
For I am Dalia, the Warrior–my legacy–love and no fear to face.

Love and Laughter always, Dalia

The Beach

What a wondrous day!
What pleasures are coming my way
The wind stroking my face
The rhythm of the waves keeping pace

My eyes soaking in pleasure
So profound, intoxicating beyond measure

The good of life surrounds me
Remembering all of it–gratitude–is the key
And I shall live 40 more good years
To help the world shed fewer tears

So I can conquer my fears And change my own tears
To the joy of giving others
For all those to come and be mothers

So Lord, give me your strength and I promise faith and fortitude
And tile world can rejoice, by the magnitude
Of each individual that is no longer destitute
Who helps to change that which can be changed
And make our world less estranged
From our love to each other
And the commitment you have asked us to give one another

Love and Laughter always,
Dalia

A Thought

To think about the wonders of all that surrounds us,
We must think of them, as intended, without a great deal of anxiety or fuss,
We are borne into this world without instruction or direction,
Our journeys filled with passing events echoing reflection.
Our birth never questioned, our purpose as we live but one,
To find our way, to search and pray, until our will is done.

So many things that could be better, had we just understood,
So many things that could have been different, if we only just could
Hindsight always twenty-twenty, lessons learned the hard way,
As we grow and learn and live, forever we experience what we must every day,
Is it by the will of God, or destiny yet to be explained?
Are there always things that must be lost, or always must be gained?

To live our lives without visions or dreams of magnificent deeds,
Is to live empty and forlorn, meeting only our basic needs,
There is no other explanation, no other guiding light,
Our entire race involved in continuous fight or flight,
But always searching for what is more than just to survive,
Always following those that have a purpose, a mission far beyond the one just to be alive.

So rejoice in the day to day, but find a passion that will move you to the core,
It is the answer to your every question, and the power to make you soar,
For each of us has the ability to reach for the top of the world, for anything we desire,
Beyond the fears and the phobias, and all that may stop us,–it will inspire
Our deepest emotions, our right to succeed and rise,–not succumb!
And let us be all that our incredible passion can create, and become,

That light, that spirit, that strength,–etched deep in our mind,
It is what separates the 'being' from the person, and helps each one of us find,

That our lives are but our deeds wrapped in pride and good will,
That our growth is measured in actions that fill,
The eternity, the Heavens, as we continue our journey through space,
And leave behind a legacy to our children, a better world now to face!

Each action building a foundation more powerful than the evil we fight,
Each bit of good gaining the momentum to overcome our plight,
Each new 'believer' creating new passion, new force,
And rejuvenating the efforts to strengthen our course,
For there is no alternative to lose, there is no choice,
We are the good, the mighty, and are all together, God's voice.

Love and Laughter always,
Dalia

My dedication to tomorrow

As I sit and reflect on days gone by,
I breathe deeply in, begin to type, and sigh,
Is there a reason or rhyme for the way events unfold?
Questions always, yet my story is still in the making, still untold.
I know that my life has deep meaning, touching many I meet, or those that read,
That my writing may someday grasp a heart, and may sow a seed,

For my readings are meant to stir,.. to reach and remind,
That our lives are surreal,–although different, we are all the same kind,
Our desires, our needs, our reasons for living,–the same,
We are here but a short time, a mission–not a game,
Yet we are children of the world, that must sing and love and live, We are meant to fulfill our destinies, and with that–give.

Give of ourselves, to others, to all those that wander into our path
Give nothing more than affection, sincerity,–offset the world's wrath.
For the fight is always here, evil and good in each a part,
Embroiled in our being, the raging waves ebb and flow in our heart,
For that is what separates us from all other kind,
And will continue to challenge every person of every year for mankind.

So live–and dedicate yourself to the path of gratitude,
Do not hesitate to love, to live, to be good..
Time ticks mercilessly away,,, aging each moment that was once so new
And forget not to see the magic of those moments, the colors–the hew,
And live like you have no tomorrow, as many of us will not,
And live and forsake all sorrow,–do not let the spirits rot,

We are here but a short time,–cherish it, hold it dear,
Live if fully, with intensity and without caution, without fear,
And strive to sense direction, the flow of whatever you are meant to be,
And remember, above all, that you only have today, no guarantee, That tomorrow will dawn anew, and life will be good,
For many, it will not, and ashes will replace where they once stood.

Love and Laughter always,
Dalia

Fleeting moments

Here again, like so many times before
Travelling on this airplane, people and mayhem galore!
All talkative or reflective, looking out the window at the past
Worlds apart so many strangers going home at last

We so often forget to focus or care
That our lives are passing, it seems so unfair
But there is always a reason that we go where we must
As we grow and mature, we learn to listen and trust
Our internal guide–our feelings and hearts
As God has provided so much of our 'smarts'

So feel strong and confident in all that you do
As life has meaning as long as we live and are true
To what we believe is our mission and core
As our spirits grow and radiate forever more.

Love and Laughter always,
Dalia

Another Year

Another year has quietly come and gone, awaiting one to be born,
This day of reflection can often lead us silent and forlorn,
As we look at what we have done, and all what we have not,
My expectations always high, the feelings in my gut,
Always wanting to have achieved, to have done so much more,
Always trying to make things right, to mend what I think I tore ...

So I look to the heavens, to my Lord, to my inspiration,
Knowing deep down that I am quite human, sometimes filled with strife and hesitation.
Yet, the new day, another chance to leave my mark, to revere in life so grand
Another day to explore the world, every crevasse of this great land,
To act like a bold brush and paint with every color of the rainbow, To travel and prance, or meander, like the streams that gently flow.

Why not try, Why weep and cry?
This day should not be the 'mourning', but the reflection–the beginning,
It should bring resolution of what we can be, of the magic, of our 'winning',
After pondering and reviewing all that has led us to be who we are,
Experience, my friend, is the precious teacher that carves our way, our star.

Never to be erased, often not to be understood,
We cannot allow ourselves to be tortured by memories often to be forgotten, if we just could.
Each story living in a part of our thoughts or dreams,
Often etched in our hearts, and stored forever, it seems ..
The better ones always to be brought to our attention,
The bad ones should teach the lessons–that is their intention ..

So as I pray to start this year anew with thoughts so pure,
Yet reminisce on past experiences filled with excitement and allure,
I reflect on all the things I still do not have complete,
And know I would want my imperfections yet to beat,

And spend the day in prayers and void of any other needs,
This cleansing of the soul important to rid the doubts and concentrate on good deeds,
And so the year is fresh, my mind abounds with songs to be sung, And I move with the rhythm of one feeling yet so young ..
I will beat the 'bad' guys, the wrongs of this world,

Who says we can't, we are the hero's of the stories as they unfold!
Each one of us borne with an incredible talent and gift,
Each one of us creating wonderful moments that always uplift.
All the world in turmoil, yet if I look very close,
The true magic and harmony is silently happening, never verbose,

The day–to–day clutter, the day–to–day hum,
The beginning of a new year, a chance to stretch each part, once numb,
And stand tall in the wonders of life so precious,
And offer help in joy, that alone–so infectious,
As to make the difference to something, to someone,
And live each day living our best, improving, until our work, our life, is done.

Love and Laughter always,
Dalia

Here and now

The days roll by, moment by moment, in a continual stream,
Our work, our schedule, parading by like an endless dream..
So we often forget that we will not be here for an eternity,
So often we look to the future, and ponder our destiny..
So often, it seems we do not stop to live that moment of the 'here and now',
And take for granted that we have only to feel, and ask not the 'why and how'.

I retrospect about myself, my heart, my feelings,
I take a breath and wonder about the success of all my healings, I am
constantly struggling to define my eternal mind,
Is that what I should be doing, and in that will I ever find?
Does anyone know the threads that strengthen, that make us really feel
whole, Does it take a perfect life to ensure that everything
we do is in our own control?

Afterall, we all seem to reflect on issues that evolve from our conception,
We all suffer from the wounds of time, as only defined by our individualized
perception.
The first part of our lives growing through the experiences of our childhood,
The second part, often, working to undo its grasp, if we just could.
Is that just a part of our inherent nature, the winding road of life we take?
Is the struggle with our ghosts eternal, ingrained in our souls, impossible to shake?
Interesting, isn't it–the answers never to be found outside ourselves,
Elusive and overwhelming, yet we continuously look for ways to
unravel and delve,
We search within the consciousness of our minds, or is it our souls?
We keep looking for that magical place and make it part of our goals,
We spend a great deal of our years in agitation and turmoil,
Hmmm … is it worth the cost of the beauty of the moments that we foil??
Take heed, and look outside the windows of your thinking,
Imagine and rejoice, life's its own magic, but it passes as we are blinking!
Revel in every precious moment, every precious person we are blessed to meet,

Understand that life's teachings include each and every one of those moments we greet,
And as you look around and breathe in those wondrous moments you now recognize,
You begin to understand–that magic?
Well, it's here and now, no longer in disguise!

Love and Laughter always,
Dalia

Paths

The wind touches my face in a gentle,
loving way I sit still, yet restless as with it I sway,
How is it–1–a creature of such power and force,
Can get caught up in a dark and tortuous course?
That imprisons my soul and leads me astray?
How can my unbound energy and strong resolve
Become entangled in hurt and bitter hearts that dissolve?
My fortitude, and leaves me with so much remorse?

The answers are whispered through the wind and earth
That caresses my body and rejuvenates my heart
And washes over all that I am and feel and grow
And cleanses with tears that are shed by all that know
That it is God's way to teach and repair
After we have reached endless moments of despair.

I stretch and search for wisdom every day
And know that there must, always must, be away..
And I strive to leave my mark on this fascinating earth
As each day slowly unfolds into a glorious birth
Of new and wondrous moments and synergy
United with the universe in harmony.

Love and Laughter always,
Dalia

Hope for the Present

I wake to a cool and overcast day
I feel forlorn and subdued, reflecting the gray,
Where is the sun, the magic, the absolute fire?
Where is the energy, the life, the incredulous desire?
I know that each day is not the same creation,
I know that it is I, not the world that must bring forth the elation.

I reach deep into my soul, covered and hidden away,
We all live our lives in 'neutral', at times led astray,
Afraid to bring out what can be so vulnerable, so dear
Afraid to touch or be touched by anyone far or near,
It is a dichotomy of emotions so intense, so unique,
It is what makes us so different and adds to the mystique.

Yet we long to be something special, something profound
We have needs and desires that reach farther than the earth we are bound,
We strive to achieve goals forged deep in our minds,
Unrelated to food, water or shelter that binds,
Everyone of us, the same,
To survive in the brilliant flame,
Of life, of love, of needs deep within the bodies that frame.

So we travel the path of such wondrous life, unaware,
That along the road weaving, and all that we think to dare,
There are stones that hurt, flowers that inspire, many chapters that unfold
There are lessons learned, and successes achieved if we are bold,
We reflect often, and sometimes see what can be the light,
We cannot but realize that we can dream and accomplish, be it day or night.

Whatever happens, we have all the tools in our possession,
We can reach deep inside ourselves, whether in fleeting, or as an obsession,
We encounter times that stop us, and shake our foundation,
We look around and find the road strewn with parts of our own creation,

And those moments become the most important as we realize our worth,
Realize that we can do whatever we want, we can recreate our birth.

As these impart our true believe, those moments that can be love or grief,
Understanding what we want to be, or find those that share our circle–The key
Those tidbits of life, of hope, of deep revelations,
Of the most important emotions that tantalize, of raw sensations Become
those defining moments, those images that bear all we have done,
That keep us moving forward, and fulfill our needs and remind us what we have won,

Our right to grow, to be who we want to be,
The right to dream, to care to feel deep, and so to be free,
That hope no longer a desire, a ghost,
The realization that it can be what we want the most,
The now, the present, living it every second of the day,
It is not the future, it is our life, to be lived in every way.

Why hope or dream! It is no longer an illusion,
No longer bound by sketchy feelings or cloaked in confusion,
We live with a reason, always to grow
The stones and flowers garnish the way to help us know,
We should feel special and embrace who we are,
Yesterday, today and tomorrow a legacy to ourselves, the true star.

Love and Laughter always,
Dalia

Give it meaning

Life is such wondrous event full of sorrow and pleasure,
An oxymoron of feelings that cut deep beyond measure.
A torrential storm that can sweep away the very meek,
A motley mixture of sensational happiness, and devastating lows so bleak,
As to bring the strongest of mankind to their knees so weak.

Why is it our destinies to learn our paths through suffering and pain?
Why cannot the way be spewed with flowers and sugar cane?
Will the lessons not be taught, will our minds not ruminate?
Will every day not be a myriad of thoughts to contemplate,
Every path to chose, every decision to review,
Every life one lives touches all the others, as though on cue.

So it is with all the pleasures and the pain I am learning to mark,
Teaching my mind to focus on the dream I wish to ignite and spark
To the future of the many that await my decision to do…
What has been my desire for oh so many years, not few
And count on my strength to overcome my indecision and disarray
Knowing full well that I am capable of achieving it–today.

My dream, my homes, my unbound energy to cultivate and give,
Choices we all make can affect how we live..
My chose is my strength, my happiness, my glory,
It is the path I will walk, it is the chapter of my story,
It is the path I will walk, it is the chapter of my story,
As I walk into the second half of my time since my birth,
The greatest of deeds must be done while still on this earth.

Take heart, my friends and all those that share my fate,
Take notice as I take charge of my life and march to create
The image I project so many times over in my mind,
Of a place no one has, a place full of laughter and acts of kind,
A place I will call home, and surrender all my worries and fears
And rejoice in the magic of many more moments to wipe away all those tears.

Love and Laughter always, Dalia

Bridges to Cross

Life is never straight and seamless, more often so unclear
Always bending and twisting, winding and hissing, full of challenge and fear,
A maze of ever complex dos and don'ts,
External and internal wants and wont's,
Each day to face with so many different levels of needs and desire,
Of basic survival, and emotions that often burn like fire,

So is it as we grow and age,
As we sense the complexity, and try to deal with each phase,
We instructively cross the many bridges looming in our sighs,
Never to understand the full value of our days and nights,
And only sometimes pondering the importance of what we do,
Is it of value, and if so, to who?

What impact do I have on the world that surrounds me?
If I am not rich or famous, what legacy will be left for all to see?
For there is a reason for all of us, I am sure,
No one lives without 'touching' someone, rich or poor,
It is inevitable,–it is written as we all travel down that path,
Experiencing the full range of emotions–, of gain and loss, of love and wrath.

We cross those bridges, the invisible ones of our minds,

Having dealt with torrid rivers of trauma and healing of all kinds,
Silently waiting for someone to lead, to explain all we want to know,
To tell us the purpose, and calm us as we grow,
Is there a spirit outside of the one we possess inside?
Or is it in our mind, always there to lead, always if we fathom,–a silent guide?

We should gain strength in our own resolve, our own fortitude,
We are the champions of our own making, never truly destitute,
As we journey and learn and experience, all those bridges, as we must,
Believe in our powers, our incredible abilities that we should inevitably trust,

Take a deep breath, and inhale the immense feeling of pride and glory,
You have done it.. you always will,–it is your destiny, and each person's story!
Rise to the occasion, do not hesitate or flaunt the power within,
Let it move you to embrace the strength of the Giant you've always been,
The path we all desire through the years that whirl right by,
The fire, or even embers, of the passions that never die,
But wait for us to awaken the thoughts that cry for release,
And finally live with truth in our hearts, and all that symbolizes our peace.

Love and Laughter always,
Dalia

'Busyness'

Awake, awake… and begin the day, Each one of us hurrying to partake in the fray,

What has happened to our life, to the magic, to the wonder We seem to have lost touch with joyful bliss, instead we ponder,

We all scurry and run at a frenzied pace, But we are rushing–to what? We all end up at exactly the same place!

The intention of our life… really, do we know what it is? Amazing, that whatever we do, it still remains a quiz?

Does it matter that throughout days there are endless chores,

How important are the feats we perform if the spirit knows not why it soars?

When was the last time you looked in the mirror–at you, When did you last 'touch' your feelings and 'tasted' life anew?

Do not let your life pass by–it would be so incomplete

Do not miss its importance–not measured in success or defeat, All our lives, our lessons, our work, our play

They are nothing more than discoveries to find our way, A divine playground to develop our inner selves, the 'I',

A wondrous fantasy borne in endless moments that never die

Allow nothing to strike that spirit, its best yet to unfold, With countless memories, but so many stories yet untold,

Forge the way, embrace every moment as the gift it is meant to be,

Encounter every person knowing they have a purpose and a part of your destiny,

Your presence, intended for this world, and this time, Forever remembered, long after you have passed your prime.

At the end of each day, no different than the sunrise,

Soak in the moments, the sunset just as spectacular a prize.
As we continue to follow the paths farther yet…
Our riches in memories of past events and people we met… Our lives now governed by deeper feelings and sense, And the clarity borne of finding such peace so immense
It should not come to pass only in the twilight of our years, We finally understand the essence of the faith that calms our fears,
It should be understood and felt by all those living the stories To savor the love of life, and not indulge the worries,
To soak in every precious ember of the spark of life, our soul,
And celebrate, and experience every second that is given to us and fulfill our role.

Love and Laughter always,
Dalia

Common Sense is Not Common

I have often toyed with writing about 'sense' in books
Incredible examples abound if one just looks
Why is it that we have expressions that totally confound?
Where is it written that raining cats and dogs does not astound?
So many phrases that defy any meaning, any sense
So many phrases that have absolutely no relevance,

So I have decided that it is time to recognize these and other cases,
As beyond phrases, there are situations that amazes,
Why do people not think as they engage their minds,
Why can we not apply 'wisdom',–there is, indeed, all kinds
The natural, the common, the intelligent, the experience,
The so many forces that confound us, as what is more important–appearances.
We are endowed with intelligence but do not apply,
Things such as charging the same price for new and old,–will defy,
Why do we not punish those who drive so darn slow?
Only punish those that speed too fast–when both change the flow?

Why do we not have items in our homes that match our size?
Our sinks too short or too tall, our toilets too low, or too small–no compromise?
Once again, too complex–so many things to surmise
So that book will be written and possible options to explore
As we move through this world, there are options galore

So–curious I am–to find out the answers to senseless and queer,
If they exist, and if they invoke laughter or tear
That is a goal, a real one–I commit
And know that it will be done, as well as it will be fit
And will be funny and sad, as many would expect
And I can't wait for the expressions it will effect.

Love and Laughter always,
Dalia

Time

Can you define what time is?
Can you tell me what it means?
Individually, it must be scrutinized and measured
And every one of us identifying what is treasured
It is only truly measured through tears of sorrow or absolute joy,
It is the etchings of so many of our happenings and scenes.
It is the special moments in our lives that we hurt or enjoy.

Time passes quickly if our spirits soar with happiness
It passes not at all when we are miserable, under stress,
Time is but a rhythm that life reflects,
A eat that continues eternally whether one accepts or rejects,

It is important to some and less to others who care
It is, however, the same for all of us in some share
Time will not stop whether we fly or fall
It does not care if we just exist or have answered the call
For it is for us alone to create its meaning
For us to understand the path and its gleaning
For us to grow our spirits and love
And remember that time is gift from the one above.

Love and Laughter always,
Dalia

Phases Of our Lives

Phases of our lives

Here again, another chapter to write, to know
The ever evolving kaleidoscope of my life as I evolve & grow,
Amazed that I feel unaccomplished, and yet ever the momentum moves me forward,
I have not achieved the special comfort of peace in my soul or heart,
As I continue to be afflicted by nights in thoughts too deep,
Thoughts that defy the solace of peaceful dreams, dancing serenely into sleep.

I know I am better, stronger, and much more in control of my being,
I am still fighting my own needs to identify the body I am seeing,
But my identity–who I am and whom I am willing to be–has emerged,
I am a kind, honest and soulful person,–lies from my life, I have purged.
Not judging, not condemning, forgiving and loving,
With desire to be with my loved ones and friends,–warmth I am coveting.

I do not wish to live alone, but I will not be dependent
I am here to help all I can, and bring kindness to those who need, at least a bit of it.
I am still not sure how solid I am in my accomplishments, my personal life,
But not willing to continue a life that is destined for strife,

And of course, a new job and a new chapter to contend with, day to day
Although I am settling into it with a bit more ease and can say,
That I have also made time for new skills, new challenges, And those speak to my heart, and fulfill my dreams and balances.

So I know that my journey continues, the road ahead yet unclear,
I long for the time to play, and frolic, and hear,
The sound of my son, surrounded by laughter and song,
And a place I call my own, and a feeling that I truly belong.
But,–in all our lives, we need to fulfill our needs and dreams wherever we are,

With the knowledge that each day may be the place we thought was yet, afar.
We must revere in life's magic,–indeed it is true,

It is in each day, in each whisper of the wind, and the beauty of the ocean so blue,
That we find our lives, our mission and the blessings we search to find
And a life that is meaningful, that is that one of a kind
Enjoy each moment, as our spirits live and roam,–the magic is to do it with unheralded kindness, warmth, and a loving face.

Love and Laughter always,
Dalia

Transitioning

It is hard to fathom a career must end when so much has been 'sown' It is not the way it shown be as my heart is heavy and turned to stone To leave when success finally achieved and those efforts obvious to be rewarded.
Why is it not the fair and the right that prevail,–not the feeling of being thwarted?
How can I not grieve when so much of my life was intertwined in that mission?
"To succeed, the President said, would guarantee benefits and gratitude to fuel my ambitions,

So it is with deep regret that I left what I knew so well,
My pride intact, if only that to take from the turmoil and stench of political Hell, There should be someone that promotes honor and teamwork, not dissension,
There must be a time when I will be worth more than just a 'mention'
And the Division created will grow healthy and strong,
Since there are so many cherished people working for the right, not he wrong

Regrets, I have many as most of us do
We live our lives with lessons that teach us to grow and become anew,
No sense to linger in the then and the 'why's"
The Important part is that we grow with integrity, and never indulge in the lies,
I have come to cherish those that do, and I for one, chose to help embrace,
The concept that it can be done, that we live in grace

I look at my past , the company that grew this girl, and challenged her core,
Bitter moments and questions abound, true, but will gradually lose their allure,
I cannot find the answers, that lies somewhere in the company's foundations
And I am not certain there will ever be courage enough to change that creation,
But I know that I will look back and find the many good things too I have so much of my heart left in what I remember in all that I do.

So I wish those I worked with well, most that crossed my path these so many years,
I was deeply touched and will cherish the memories and shed many tears,
I have learned many lessons and will not forget all I learned,
Another chapter to begin, and write on the one left, and new markets to find, Knowing that my mark has been made, and I will remain at this company, one of a kind.

Love and Laughter always,
Dalia

Birthdays

It is amazing how time does fly!
And the moments of our lives seemingly flowing by,
There is nothing more paramount than the moments we make,
Yet so few of us really understand what in life, we take–
Not the material, not the property or money that will give us the thrill,
But the enrichment of spirit and soul that so deeply fulfill,
So as this year's light flickers to an end,
And the dawn of a new one peaks through the bend,
It is important to take note, to remember and reflect
About all those moments that we may often neglect
And the incredible feelings that we should treasure,
For life is wondrous, and incredible beyond measure!
Have a wonderful birthday, and great year to come,
Filled with all that you desire and wish to become..
And do not forget that all we really need to do and be
Is whatever we chose, although we cannot foresee
What the future will hold, and what will unfold

Enjoy what each day unveils, as if it is a gift
Filled with a spectrum of feelings to uplift
Your mind and spirit on your journey through time
And be grateful for your health and happiness, after all, you are in your prime.

Love and Laughter always,
Dalia

Storm, Sun & Rainbows

Our paths intertwined, our hearts aligned,
That is the way it was meant to be,–and for all to see,
We met, we laughed, we shared, we dared–and planned,
It was so right… so great, yet troubled, we knew risky,–banned,
With so much at risk, and with unbound love and devotion,
We struck out on a journey of complex worlds and deep emotion.

Storm, Sun & Rainbows–that is what we created,
A world of the highest highs, and lowest lows, and love unabated,
A world of two strong individuals, uncompromising and stubborn,
Two strangers of intense and unyielding natures,
looking for the unison to be born,
It should have been clear–to live together should be happiness always,
and never to be,
Hurtful, spiteful, harmful, and harsh, as many couples evolve–eventually.
Storm, Sun & rainbows, a mixture of volatility and emotions and love so strong,
A concoction that is unlike any other, and could be right or could be wrong,
Few in this world can profess to have lived or loved with so much intensity,
Few would have dared to share the excitement, or be challenged by its immensity,
Yet we stood in that hallway,–the one carved by love, by desire,
And fueled by the want of a life of happiness and love that should never tire..
Storm, Sun & Rainbows–the highest highs, the unbearable lows,
That has been our legacy,–our lives full of moments of love that flows,
Yet dark days of pain and hurt that burns down to my core,
And ripped into my heart and into the love it bore,
And inflicted the doubt that replaced what was once so pure,
Drowning so much of it, that all I could do was pray for a cure.
Storm, Sun & Rainbow–our lives still in turmoil,
Cali you find the answer that will change this course, and foil?
What is destructive, to bring back the magic that should never ever

disappear, What is draining, where once our spirits soared, and never was there a tear?
What will be the change, can the love so strong survive?
Should not the magic of such intensity be the guide, for this love to revive?

The answer–to reach deep into the hearts that knew so much joy and ease,
That laughed, that loved, that frolicked with little care, the moment to seize,
And rediscover, redefine … to forge a unison, real, true, divine…
That is the only way.. nothing else to say,
Our paths so clear, both strong, my fear to be alone, and missing the touch,
But not to live in pain, that is worse, and hurts so much.
Storm, Sun & rainbow … the intensity, the glow, the fire..
Today dimmed by lack of trust, of ambiguities, so much that I tire.
Yet knowing that the sparks yet alive, can re–ignite beyond the strife,
And hope that the future can be reborne, a new day, a new life,
And what was once our dream, be our future, our new way,
And let the rainbow flow inside our soul, and be remembered every day.
That is the choice,–for two people never to hurt, and always to share,
To be friends, to trust, to understand each soul;–to care,
Two people who need to never want the other to hurt or cry,
And always protect the depth on their trust, and not to vie,
To put egos aside, and live forever together in ease and wonder,
That is what must be, or forever to live in the past and ponder,
I look forward to that day that answers will fill our heart,
And bring back the magic, and keep us from being apart.

Love and Laughter always,
Dalia

Forever Searching

It seems such a short time that I have lived, yet I sense that I am in my prime.
Not yet having reached my goals, for they are many; but determined to,– before my time,
I have reached an awareness that betrays my frustration–understanding it all Hard to imagine I have so much to offer, and so damn smart,– how many times did I fall?
I love life as few people do,–in appreciation so many miss in everyday hustle, I reach for the stars, and driven to accomplish so much,–more than I will achieve but so much more than others strive to try,
So I continue my path and struggle to find ways to slow so much of my hustle,
I continue to work, and work, and work, but know that my time to be,
Something new,–unique,–that will bring happiness, and peace in knowing why.
How much I cherish these many moments!
They fulfill my soul through the love I feel–the closeness to my son, and my family, and friends
How much I look to so many more of these days, as I long to be that more, and find what happens when this part of my journey ends
NO.. not in death, but as one chapter closes and another unfolds, Not that I have regretted EVERYTHING, some–yes,,
but finally knowing I understand my 'core',
It seems I strengthened, as we all must, when we have fallen; yet achieve success
overcoming the worse,–and somehow live on as never before.
Yes, happiness is indeed within,–a lifetime event that evolves only from one's own self–worth and awareness.
Yes–we all have that ability, that need, the desire,–that IS our destiny. Only 'we' have the chance to find our ways, frolic in love and energy

And thrill in the sensations borne as moments of carelessness.
Remember as you grow, and learn, and love and hurt, and ultimately
search–It is what makes us what we are, and how we learn WHO we are
If we live and learn and finally find the internal vision of what you see from afar,
That is all,–the important lesson at the end of the path,
For the road has begun for the soul that now shares that spirit without wrath, And brings unto the world a reason to smile,
Yet another chapter to remind us our world is not so vile,
Yet another chapter for our children to begin the cycle as we have,
And ultimately, have brought the whole of mankind to a better life, We learn that we each have a purpose, a reason to be,
And leave the world some wonder, some mark, some part of our legacy.
Live, and love and smile and live,
And never a moment forget that our brightest moments are those we give..
Love and Laughter always, Dalia

What is next

What will happen this year, and those yet to come?
I am so committed to changing this world, and not to succumb,
To losing my dreams, my hopes and desires,
To embrace the passion, the burn, those images that fuel my fires,
I know how much I can give, I can offer, I can serve,
I know that I would like to 'save' what I can, so many that deserve,

I am not alone in these needs, in this quest, in that journey,
Some of us continue to dream and continue in that for eternity,
I am not waiting,–I cannot, my spirit will die
I have too much inside to feel, to heal, to grow, to answer why,
This year will change what I feel inside already shifted
I have made a switch, in my heart, in my soul, a veil uplifted,

Both in my work, and my open mind and heart,
I have healed, am still healing, but look forward to my future to chart,
I am determined to expose my dream, my ambition
I cannot wait as life offers every one of us a chance to be a magician
And beyond those things that surround us, that fill,
We also need those special feelings, that affection, that chill
I am also ready to share, to explore, to touch
And to express feelings that every one needs so much,
Knowing the follies and fortunes of the journey behind,
We all must make sense of it, and intimacy, find,
This phase is exciting, it must be deep, and true, yet surreal,
I write this with a smile, as life is as magical as it is real.

Love and Laughter always,
Dalia

Count the Many

Count the many good days, not the ones full of stress
Count the wonderful golden moments–not any that seem meaningless,
Count the nights full of stars, not the ones washed in rain,
Count on the power of your loved ones, not the careless ones that caused you pain
Count on the meaning of hope, not the meaning of despair
Count on knowing that there is always a way, and be grateful for all those that care

Count the colors of the rainbow, not the dark hues of depression,
Count the wonders of children playing, not those of aggression,
Count the blooming of the flowers, not the falling of their leaves,
Count the thrill of trying something new,–do not worry what it achieves,
Count the blessings of the path of life, not of all its fears,
Count each moment of that life by its many smiles, not by all its tears.
Count all the delicious morsels, not the ones that leave an awful taste
Count all the magical smells and joyful sights that give us pleasure, not the ones we waste!
Count the wondrous growth of our children, not the havoc they can create,

Count those moments as precious, and a gift that is our fate…
Count all that you hold incredulous, not the aches and pains along the way
Count the joys that God created and the beauty of each and everyday…
Above all, remember who you are, not who you may have been,
Remember all the good you can impart, not the things you consider 'sin',
Remember that our lives are but the lessons, not the final judgement yet to be,
Remember that you are here to be your best, yet we struggle to finally see,
That, after all, we count on the magic of our being, not the day to day,
And count, as we must,–to make peace with ourselves, and revel in the joys along the way.

Love and Laughter always,
Dalia

What to say

It is the New Year, a time to renew
I am in the skies again, flying home one more time,
Bone tired, with little energy, and words so few,
And the knowledge that I am not getting younger, definitely in my prime.

What to show for it? What have I done?
Working on so many things to accomplish, but trying with that, to have fun,
Hard to do when there is no time, and deadlines abound,
Hard to reflect when the work never stops, and rest is a desire so profound,
So, as I indeed have time to reflect on a life full of strife and in conclusions,
It also suggests that there is more to do, and to each of us, our own illusions,
To roam, to romp, to look for ways to live without constraints
To find solace in knowing that we are not alone in that space, that magic
that life so often paints

I have searched for so many years to find exactly what?
When I know that it is the everyday that is the magic in itself,
It is that very point we all so often miss until the end.

And often struggle to really feel when turmoil attends
That space is ours, we can chose not to let those feelings guide our decisions,
And forever nurture the core of our being,
To capture the many magical moments of splendor–to fulfill the true breath
of our visions.

Love and Laughter always,
Dalia

Today

There is the birth like the sun rise of every day we live,
And then. there is the end, like dusk of that same day, I believe
Precious moments, so many, so rich and bright,
They are like sprinkles of magic for us to savor and delight!

What a strange thought, you read and wonder!
I must be seeing this day in a different world, you ponder!
Not every day that we live is beautiful and true,
There are days when we are so melancholy and blue!

No, my friend, it is not so by design..
The life we have is very, very divine.
It is our minds, alas, that we must refine,
That work to interpret the days as our thoughts define..

Yet, the worst of our experiences cannot suppress,
The beauty around us and those touches that caress,
We have only to capture the sight, not only to see,
We have only to energize from the touch, not only to be..
Today is no longer–, leaving only the slightest of imprints behind,
Tomorrow will be borne,–take a moment and so remind,
Yourself and all others of the joy and sweet taste,
And be grateful for the precious moments,–do not haste.

We are what we chose, through that world in our mind,
We can fret and worry and be angry, not kind,
But at the end of the birth and death of our wondrous days,
All that will matter will be the spirit that stays,
Ever more rich and ever so much stronger,
Grateful for all it had experienced and yearning no longer…

Love and Laughter always,
Dalia

Chapters to be written

My mind churns, endlessly processing 'data' from this body and soul It never rests,–never ceases to work,–that is its role,
The it–the I–a constant question, as all our minds work the same–or do they,
We are souls,–not robots that as we act and ponder–living individual creations,
Amazing more, the years that pass, as we live more, and learn more
We sift through this mind, for answers, for help–to find our core,
We live experiences, good ones, and horrible ones–and yet live on
Are we then smarter, brighter, wiser, happier, content?
Is there a formula, some way, that someone may someday invent?
All of us on these paths,–all will end in the energy we become,
It would be so much easier,–as we sometimes vanish in numb,
Easier to 'disappear' than deal with oneself, or the hurt,
Knowing it is you, the individual, the mind being overt
And then, the other side–of running and hiding,–buzzing and busy
As we cannot find the 'self' at peace if we stopped being dizzy
No answers today, but the stories of all of us are not even yet told,
We must look at all we have done, good deeds and bad, and not fold,
We must strengthen our powers to understand that mind–and where we are,
As we are like books being written, the author–the editor,–the star
We have the gift of life, mostly forgotten in the day to day,
We must stop, and look, and feel and touch,–through the fray,
And imagine for a moment,–each day–how life's beauty, and friends, and family convey
The love in our hearts, and the mind's fear allay
We are writing pages each day we live,–the way we act, the way we feel,
We should count our blessings, and laugh and smile–it IS a big deal
We are our own masters of attitude, of happiness and joy,
We are also those that can make those less fortunate be able to enjoy
By sharing what may–material, or wealth or time or poems,
As we do, you will see that our minds slow the churn, and the mutter,
As we find our way to more serenity of who we are, and rid the clutter

So indeed–write, on paper or in that power of the mind,
And decide only to focus on the good parts–and you will find
The chapters become more beautiful, more real,
And the world that surrounds you, surreal.

Love and Laughter always,
Dalia

My Dreams
Give it meaning

Life is such a wondrous event full of sorrow and pleasure,
An oxymoron of feelings that cut deep beyond measure.
A torrential storm that can sweep away the very meek,
A motley mixture of sensational happiness, and devastating lows so bleak,
As to bring the strongest of mankind to their knees so weak.
Why is it our destinies to learn our paths through suffering and pain?
Why cannot the way be spewed with flowers and sugar cane?
Will the lessons not be taught, will our minds not ruminate?
Will every day not be a myriad of thoughts to contemplate,
Every path to chose, every decision to review,
Every life one lives touches all the others, as though on cue.

So it is with all the pleasures and the pain I am learning to mark,
Teaching my mind to focus on the dream I wish to ignite and spark,
To the future of the many that await my decision to do..
What has been my desire for oh so many years, not few
And count on my strength to overcome my indecision and disarray
Knowing full well that I am capable of achieving it–today.

My dream, my hopes, my unbound energy to cultivate and give,
Choices we all make can affect how we live..
My chose is my strength, my happiness, my glory,
It is the path I will walk, it is the chapter of my story,
As I walk into the second half of my time since my birth,
The greatest of deeds must be done while still on this earth.

Take heart, my friends and all those that share my fate,
Take notice as I take charge of my life and march to create
The image I project so many times over in my mind,
Of a place no one has, a place full of laughter and acts of kind,

A place I will call home, and surrender all my worries and fears
And rejoice in the magic of many more moments to wipe away all those tears.

Love and Laughter always, Dalia

Family & Friends & More

My Son

My son, my joy, my hopes and dreams–
My thoughts, my life–my blood that streams
How interesting that I yearn for all those years,
Filled with so much laughter–and sometimes a few tears
All in all–I raised you full of pride,
However much I missed due to consequence and life's tide,

How I pray you understand the many why's and reasons
That will keep you close to me and know I'll be there for all seasons.
Dear one–you are so much the light that keeps my hopes and dreams so Strong,
How I hope that you will take my soul, and know that your mom, all Along,
Is a warrior for your heart and mind
And a mom who loves you, with feelings of a special kind
And looking to be the best,
And pushing to excel, and will not rest..

Yet, if you chose, my son to call, Whether in joy, or if you fall,
I will revel in the task to offer help ever small
That will improve your lot
Whatever, whenever–you are 'on the spot'

So grow, my son with hopes and an abundance of pleasures
And know that creation is good, yet measures
Our poise and strength and gratitude
And our journey full of challenges in multitude
Ultimately to define our character and fortitude.

Smile, my son as you read and know
That your mom, and dad, are proud and aglow
In sharing these precious moments of your life and daily flow
So grow with great joy and faith and love
Life is good, to be lived, always protected from above

And is so proud of you and all you are
And never ever, will I 'be' too far
As I forever am a part of you that will carry on all that we cherish
And with that, forever I know, that will never let my memory perish
Love you always and forever
And nudge you beyond all 'boundaries' and be with you forever and ever

Love and Laughter always,
Dalia

Mom

My dearest mom, how I love you so!
You are so previous, so sweet and so much aglow
That I imagine all the colors of the rainbow that flow
In a halo of light that explode in so much energy
And transfers from you, and becomes a part of me
For you are unique, so special so dear
You must look around and have no fear
Surely, you know that you are meant to be near
Already in my spirit, so much in my heart
That nothing, but nothing shall keep us apart
Your laughter, your smile, so real in my mind
My prayers to keep you safe and to find
That special feeling of warmth and security
In remembering that life is amazing filled with wonders to See!
Be well my mother, my friends, my deepest love

Remember that forever He will watch over you from above
And my promise to you as is the same for my son so sweet
Is to never, but never leave you alone to meet
All the challenges life brings our way to beat,

And I will rejoice in the love I feel from your warmth and special way,
Forever, my mom–I will keep you close every day.
And smile as I think of the future and how much more we can play,
And all the things I want to show you and say.
So I can give you the sun and the beach, and shoo away the Gray!

Love and Laughter always,
Dalia

Daddy

Our lives rush by as we grow so fast,
rom babies to teens to adults at last,
We take for granted that our parents so dear,
Will always be here, always be near.

So, daddy today, I am here to say,
That I remember you fondly and love you and pray,
That you have a great moments and memories each day,
And that you enjoy life to the fullest, in every way!

I wish to tell you how much I appreciate you,
Our moments together, although often too few,
And looking to see the love in your smile,
Or the warmth of your voice when we chat for a while.

So be well, my daddy, life is great,
Cherish every moment, it is our fate..
Remember how much love surrounds you,
Mom, Debbie, Zeev and especially me too,
We are here to help you from feeling 'blue'
And remind you always
With simply "I love you"…

Love and Laughter always,
Dalia

My Brother Zeev

It is hard to imagine how much time has flown,
My Bobelech and I were so close once and now grown,
We are finally reconnecting–with so much time in–between
But my brother, his heart as always, so big, never could be mean,
Not saying that his temper and his very hard life did not play a huge role
And so often in life, so much to pass and so many tough experiences,
they indeed do take their toll,
My brother, I love you–always have and always will
You watched over me when you were so young, and we had only each other still
We left to many other worlds, and lost many moments in life
And had to deal with our own journeys, and endure so much strife,
Still, my dear Bobelech, you are always in my thoughts and heart,
You are always and forever, my special brother, even when we are apart,
You should know that you can count on me for support, for any reason,
I know we have not shared everything, but you know I am here, in any season,
I love you more today than ever as I watch the hardships you endure,
With so much grace and no complaints,–how that is done,
I am not sure As I am optimistic always, and try to find the best of most

But I so admire my brother, who takes everything in stride,–to you I toast
Forever my brother, know your sis loves you deeply and as you are
MY Bobelech, my big brother, and prayers that we will not be apart, so far
And life will be easier for you, each and every day, a bit more
Peace and serenity to someone deserving, and who is loved to the depth of
my core

Love and Laughter always,
Dalia

My Sister

(before you changed and left us)

You came into our lives so small, so pale,
It was frightening to take care of something so frail,
And I so often worried that what I was supposed to do,
Would not be exactly what mothers always knew.

But we are so fortunate to have you here to enrich our life,
You have grown from a baby, to a daughter to a perfect wife…
Your spirit so beautiful, so precious, so sweet,
A joy to us all, and everyone you meet

My beautiful sister, we live so far apart,
Yet always, in fact, not too far from my heart,
Family and friends I have learned is the key
Of all we do and what is important to me.

Sisters are magical, borne with a special bond,
As the years pass, as though with a wave of a wand,
We mimic each other, and gesture the same,
As though produced in the very same name.

You have much more to do, much more to see
Many more memories, and a mother to be,
So many directions, so many paths to chose,
As long as you are healthy, you can not lose
Since no family, mates or a career,
Can quite replace you so dear..
Love and Laughter always, Dalia

Love and Laughter always,
Dalia

To My Newfound Family in New York!

Well it sometimes takes one part of a lifetime to reconnect
With those folks in your family, your realm, that it truly can affect
I knew them for a brief part of time and then, in a flash, we let them go
Why or how or reasons abound but in reality, as it is, we live and we grow
When I found you, Yoram, Marian, Steven, Sharon, the part of my true bloodline
I was so happy, thrilled, so ecstatic to know that you are there, and so very fine
All of you embraced me, as though I have been there forever and ever, And am so deeply moved that I am not alone in America and never Will allow these ties to be broken again, and truly will endeavor
To find more ways to connect, bring us closer and truly not allow our ties to sever
Even though time may pass, and I know I still may not visit enough, I do promise that I will find time however I can, regardless how rough
To visit, and hope you do too, as life is too short indeed,
But at the moment, I am not out of the workplace and have mouths to feed,
But Yoram, Marian, Sharon and Stephen,–know that you are truly loved, adored
My prayers as New Year's, Passover, Yom Kippur come yearly and we must afford
Some time to gather our thoughts and remember our loved ones new and old, And grow stronger ties as more stories and memories unfold
So to you I do promise to not let our family ties ever wain
As it was a miracle to reconnect, and this should never be in vain This poem is to remind you that you are all in my hearts and soul,
I strive to have my son Guy, never feel alone and know you better–that is my goal
For indeed, I feel blessed to know the depth of family so wonderful and kind
I feel I know that destiny and the angels above were working hard for us to bind.

Love and laughter always,
Dalia

My Special Neighbors

It is very unique that life finds special people along the path of your life
And such I know I am blessed when I found a couple during years of strife
We all can live by each other and never warm the parts of your soul
And often, and too often, those that surround your house, that is their goal
But As I was blessed, as is my son to have found a family with depth and sincere
In the love that developed and it was very very clear,
That we were meant to be friends, not for one day, but forever,
As we shared is so many good moments, hard ones and always to endeavor
To help each other and grow and preserve the love of one another
And share with it, the love of our animals–and these folks, say never bother
But for all that can be good or bad in lives many ups and downs
My dear Liz and Malcolm and Lauren–forever you have touched us, and memories abound
That day you sat with me in grief and pain in a closet on the floor
Sharing in my turmoil, in the unknown and the dark, and talking the 'what–for'
And never let me feel alone or the knowledge that someone does not care
I know that there are few and far between that one can say that–fair

But you are forever a part of us, and forever I know I will not allow us to part
And forever and ever, this precious family is in our heart
And abundance of time yet to come and many magical moments to make
SO forever Liz, Malcolm and Lauren, for heaven sake
We are bound by more than this and look forward to many
more memories and magical moments to make

Love and laughter always,
Dalia

My Close Friend Found

It is so profound that I finally started writing again, I have that feeling,
And maybe also that I have found special ones that help with my healing
Sharon, dear one, you found me in time past so far way,
My propensity to 'not remember, not recall, and stay as far away,
As I possibly could from those memories, those days, the hurts,
Yet you were there in the moments that were good, and the many that should revert,
To memories that lead me to remember that who I am is true to those days too,
And yes, the many years that passed have not changed the feeling between me and you,
It is that, that which cannot be explained as the core to our depth of love
And says to the world, that we are friends forever and meant to be from above,
It is that which lets me know that the dept of love and trust abound,
And that the fact that you searched for me and found,
Is as special a day as you will never know, and my feelings explored,
As so many of those special moments must be shared and lead to more accord,
More peace of mind, more knowing that we all have these journeys and these moments where
We should be able to say things that are not meant for everyone but should be shared,
And that dear Sharon is what you have given me along with so much

As we will continue to always and always stay in touch
Know that forever I am grateful that you reached out and found me indeed,

And that we have shared many magical moments and I want more to feed
As many of the ways that we can share more and learn and dare
To grow with each others best intentions and with care
And know that these special feelings, and love and cherished, so rare..
Love you forever and forever we will share..

Love and laughter always,
Dalia

To That Special Friend and my Cat Angel

To get on that plane unless the occasions are to make good memories and laughter galore
And share in the affection,–offer appreciation, happiness and more
So a beautiful new soul came into my life this past bit of time
With a huge personality, albeit shy and closed and a bit sublime,
A deep and thoughtful and rich plethora of emotions and affection,
Hidden deep with the walls of kittens and cats she feeds and offers immense protection
Georgette, offering advise and time and attention and more
For all those that need her, that ask as long as it is about a 'soul with fur',
She is feisty and so deep but hides that well
I tease her as she is in a 'mushroom state' and has need to open up and many tales to tell
She has become a rock in my life overflowing with so many parts and pieces
She is undeniably a piece that has become a part of my journey with all its etchings and creases
I have few deeply routed friends that stand the test of time–its stresses and strain
As we often saturate those we love with deeper hues of love and pain
It is born of fear and vulnerability in a hurtful world, and thus, few can we trust
And somehow, allow our many layers to be exposed, as we must So my precious mushroom, my friend,
Know that you are loved for all you are in every wonderful way,–to the end,
I am forever grateful and in awe of the many sides and many parts of you,
And the deep connection that has become, and that is shared with so few…
And somehow, allow our many layers to be exposed, as we must
So my precious mushroom, my bratter, my friend,
Know that you are loved for all you are in every clutsy and wonderful way,– to the end,
I am forever grateful and in awe of the many sides and many parts of you,
And the deep connection that has become, and that is shared with so few…

Love and laughter always, Dalia

My special Lupe

There exist so few people in the world today
That have hearts of gold, of souls that can share so deeply, and act like a ray Of sunshine, of hope, of inspiration, of deep feelings and strength and love She comes with so little requests and so much to give–a gift from above
Is that to say she may be an angel, someone walking among us, not human, not real?
NO, she can hurt, she has troubles, she has strife, she has hurts, and more But she does not show the hardships she endures, those she does not share As she helps you find your stride, offers support and advise and shows so much care,
She is a true friend who invited me into her heart, and her family–her core, She has become this amazing rock, and an ally and yes, a part of my heart I adore,
There are so few people that go out of their way to just listen and show
And stay with you during the hardships, during your meltdowns, and a time in need,
She is the Matriarch of her family, as dependable as she is to me, as indeed She has a soul that helps all that wander into her grace, and her circle,
She is as a light for all to know, a smile that says 'I am here', always to know You can count on her to 'hear' you–and yes I said 'hear' the depth of your thoughts,
And remember that life's many 'bumps' will pass as many more good times are sought
So Lupe, my friend, my soulmate, your family–, you are such a big part of my life
Acceptance of each and every part of you and me is a rare gift, with me you share
I love you with all my heart and forever you know, to eternity, I will care
And pray to have many more magical moments for us to laugh and frolic and play
As life's gifts are the special moments that are carved with you if we may
And to the memories that already make me smile, even as time marches on apart
Those memories remind me of the love and connection forever and ever in our hearts.
I know the days are near for us always to find time together, my goal As you are forever a part of my love, the deepest most amazing part of my soul

Love and laughter always, Dalia

To my special Friend Lori

There are many times in life where you wander through and share brief but special connection
That is the way I feel about this amazing lady, this bright light and deep affection
I have known her many years, and shares so many good days as well as fears
I have shared with her some deep and dark days and tears
As well as the history of life with family and open talk with trust and care So much of that seems so easy and not so important
as it is definitely not enough time
Yet I know in my heart, that she has touched my life into my prime
She has always listened and deeply shown affection and care
And I know, for some strange reason that I can call upon her, if I dare
She is special, and also too often that not, does not chose to share
Her hurt, her problems as she is too busy listening and being such a rare
Soul in a world of fake and not enough of a person who is real
It is with such love and affection I know that I feel
Her every word, her every suggestion, comes from a deep place of love
And we talk a great deal of the best of things, and angels up above
But that is the point, Lori is one of those that has touched my heart and is true
To all that is real, and is good and that guides her to be for you
And for me and for her friends, her family, her kids and more
So to this special person I am privileged to know and love to the core
I write these special words of affection
So she never ever forgets that she indeed, has touched me and with a connection
So strong that bonds us forever and am blessed to call a friend and more
And will hope to find time to share many moments for
our memories to love and in our hearts, to store

Love and laughter always,
Dalia

Bond of Friendship

Time passes and sometimes, those we love so much can hurt as well
I cannot say that I do not love this person who I met
and fought for me in times that felt like Hell,
My Yvonne was there when I was going through so much pain
And with her help, my spirit was lifted and I could be stronger and gain
The depth of what I knew should be the Dalia that would always find her way
And at the moment of grief, and indecision, had let her best parts stray
But as time passed, we also drifted,
In can happen as life with many of its twists and turns allow people to part
as sands are shifted
And lives go separate ways and new things happen, and new phases
Become a part of life and the memory of each other hazes
All I can hope and pray is that the depth of love and the bonds of affection
Will bring us back as we deeply felt the affection
And shares so many important memories, the good, the laughs, the stubs
The important moments of life that can only be reflected with those you love
And that will always be a part of you forever etched in your heart
So dearest one–know you are always etched and truly never meant to be
apart
As we shared so many years important to our families,
to each other and our core
And for that reason, I know that we will find each other, and will have so
many more
So many more moments, movie and magical ones to laugh and wonder
Why it took so long for us to make that happen and lay all that was asunder
As we remember that our hearts are open and loving and care
That the most important part of life is exactly that–love and so much more
to share

Love and laughter always,
Dalia

Mom's Angel

In life, there are many times to grieve, and many times to celebrate

No one wishes the passing of loved ones or to remember that date,

But in the truest form, and for the most critical of time and feeling

A man came into our lives who became an angel to support, as the family was still reeling

This man, our John, who would not ask for anything, who stood steadfast in everything required

And became the rock, mom's savior, Dalia's strongest ally and so inspired Everyone to know that he cared, he loved, and without any reason,

Became our family, one of us, and to be counted on, anytime and any season.

So is life in its many colors and hews, those of magical moments and those of ones that hurt,

We as family know those that can continue to grow and will never revert, That became John and Sharon, now our family forever and ever,

Etched into our hearts with appreciation and gratitude and ties that no one can sever

It is that which separates people from what are just ties, to the dept of love and always to be 'there'

As the ties to family, to help those in need, cannot be defined in words but each day in the actions that become how deeply these people care

So in fact we have extended our love and appreciation with borders, or time It is profound for me to know that we can make new bonds even in our prime Based on shared love and commitment to my mom, my dearest and most precious love

And knowing that this person shares those concerns that will protect her, as an angel from above

And forever will carry with that the love and adoration of both me and my son

And know that whatever we can do, will brighten their days and forever our hearts have won

Love and laughter always, Dalia

Friends

Friends are those special people that are far and few between
That walk into our lives and always mean
The very best for us without reproach or judging views
Advising in earnest their feelings of don'ts and do's.

I am blessed with such people, indeed so far and few between
That always can be trusted and care for me and are keen
To find a way to always make my troubles less the issues
And offer their love, whether I need hugs or tissues.

So, Jan my friend, and others, too
I wanted to let you know that you are cherished, nothing new!
But since each moment in our lives are special, so few
One must always find the opportunity to remember and do.
All that we want to live and say and thrive anew.

Be well, my friend and do not fret
We are in life like stars, acting out whatever we desire,
And people, so special, always ready to inspire,
And the best of them are for me as treats

Offering fortitude and support for any and all feats.
My love always for you so dear,
I pray that I can journey along knowing no fear

Love and laughter always,
Dalia

That Special Soul, Ana

8.01.2024

As life progresses and often souls come in and out
It is hard to predict when someone special comes about
Each day comes and goes with purpose if at best
And the need to capture and tame all that energy, that as our quest
And as my good luck would have it, this amazing soul wandered into my life
First at my neighbor's doorstep, with little fanfare or strife

First to help my aching body, not so much my soul
And accepting the challenge of working those areas that have taken life's toll
Her name, Ana, a special lady whose little laugh is so easy to hear
And here charm and ease of life drawing you in , have no fear
She has that heart, that language beyond those words we say
That make one feel special no matter what life has thrown your way

Ana has become more than a friend, more than that person casual in my circle,
She has become a trusted part of every day, of every thought, of every hurdle,
She helps me maneuver those challenges I normally handle alone
And does so without reference to the burden it will create for herself , amount unknown,
She is as precious as any part of the family that I now know her part to play
As I know she cares as deeply for me, as anyone who cares may display

So to the angels above who have found you for me
I am grateful for every day that I share moments that help me be carefree
Because of her guidance and discipline for my body and soul
And her special messages for my heart as well, to lighten it, our goal
And to forever build on the friendship that has become so deep
Ana, stay healthy, stay well and know that my love grows as faith does leap.

Laughter and light
Dalia

Angels

When I despair, and feel lost and wounded, I reach for them,
When I cannot find the words or actions, everything is such mayhem
When I think my soul cannot rest, I am tired, I reach for them,
When I yearn for peace and answers, and feel so heavy,–I want
Someone else at the helm,
When all I can feel is hurt, and all I feel is that I am condemned.

That is the task of the angels, those invisible spirits that are always There,
Skeptical you are? You think that they do not exist, you do not care?
Well think again, my friend.. in this world so real,
You need to find things that are true blue, and surreal..
That will not be in your job or your normal daily routine,
It will only be a part of your spirit and if your soul is serene,

How that happens is in your belief of the heart,
Where only love and giving are not too far apart,
Only true expressions of such feelings, such incredible care

Will enable the emergence of those angels, those elusive figures so rare For
they come to those who strive for some sort of good, some deeds,
Not always succeeding, but at least that soul that heeds.
What must be the case in most people's lives,
We are but humble beings, we are creatures that
It is the ultimate drive, the power the reason the rhyme,
It is the answer to all the questions, then, now and as we travel throughout time.

Love and laughter always,
Dalia

Tigers & Dragons

The flow of life is like the moving tide,
Feelings surge and swell in waves that collide,
Ever moving, ever streaming in the depth of our mind,
Our hearts ever searching for the paths that unbind,
The meaning of life, the creation of our destiny,
Untamed, unpredictable, like the seas of eternity

The quest continues in whatever paths we chose,
Some souls less troubled, some unfortunate to lose,
The meaning of life,–the treasure of each day,
As some of us ponder our journey, our way,
The better of us finding solace that our lives can enrich
Each one of us unique, each has its purpose and niche,

So is it true in the studio I have found,
A place of sweat, of pride, of energy unbound..
Here also is a place that challenges and measures,
The endless ebb of moments etched in pain or pleasures,
As we learn the art of discipline and devotion
Of achievements and growth wrapped in so much emotion.

Here, too, I have found my heart's desire to connect,
My many moments of fun and giving that affect,
Special people that return that same feelings of heart
That offer their friendship and did from the start
Of new ideas borne in ageless culture and freedom Of tigers and dragons,
representing power and wisdom,

Of rising tigers and salsa queens,
Favorite people that know what it means,
To 'be there' and lend a helping hand unrequested,
To offer encouragement and listen uncontested,

Of stretching and learning what we never knew,
How much more we are, how much more we can do,
Of 'love and light' and so much dedication,
As to give us all incredible motivation.

Love and laughter always,
Dalia

My Extended Children

It had been a lifetime when I first saw those tiny faces,
The ones I accepted when I married my man, those places
Those places we go when we marry and do not really know
What we truly must do when there are children you must grow
Not of your own womb those innocent in the change of lives
And when women change husbands, and men change wives.

It was with little preparation and with little experience as one must learn
That these wonderful little souls, they too must trust, something you earn.
Then and today, I love those wonderful souls and their families and more
As they are part of my being, a feeling that they are part of my core
My son had brothers and a sister to play with, wow–it was such a blessing
And no way was that as difficult as when I heard they were moving, no caressing
Those little faces, and the fun we had through life (ha when they threw me in the pool)
As I look back and see that it was so much love, not that I was a fool

Forever Gil, Ron and Sharon,–you are a part of us, and I pray that we will always be
That important word, that feeling, the ups and downs of family,
This poem reminds me that I need to spend more time finding out about your lives
And the same should be yours to find out about Guy and yes, what he buys
Or what you do day to day, week to week, it should be no longer
As time flies, and we do forget to check in and without checking, our bonds will not get stronger
That should be a goal–to never let go of all the good that families
Do bring and impart
And traditions, and lives and moments to remember for our families to never be so apart
That we forget, that our children grow without knowing
The love and attention and moments and kindness and bonds that should

be growing
As I write this today, and on my travels so many places every I go
I recommit to you and to Guy, and myself that I should relive the glow
Of knowing the moments I so cherish and remember about each one of you
And promise not to lose the touch, the important look, the hugs and renew
Those bonds that are unbreakable, memories that should be made
And to promise to see, to call, to remember and let not those memories fade,
And make certain that Guy, and your children, we do not fall further apart
My love to all of you and promise that we shall not do so,
and to hold each one of you in my Heart

Love and laughter always,
Dalia

Family & Friends

So what makes us what we are?
What magical force can electrify us to shine like a star?
How do we grow from something so small to stoic and tall?
In so many years, when life brings us trouble–and hurts so deep,
How do we climb out of those dark crevasses of mind and body, when the walls seem so steep?
And wrestle with all the demons in our hearts and soul and are wracked with the silent tears we weep?
There is only one answer, the family and friends that are there to share the pain,
To give the unconditional love that only can be felt with those that care–and does not wane
Those that know you, for your strengths and all you are, but also see you for what you are,
A person, fallible, vulnerable and human–but so deeply care Nothing ever can replace those that are truly 'there'
And say soothing words when there seems nothing about life that may be fair,

But life is amazing–giving us chances to love the magical moments gifted us to explore
And time to cherish those that you may take for granted and time to adore
As life is fleeting,–the moments pass in a glance
We hardly notice that as we move and never know in advance
The ebb and flow that can bring us from amazing ecstasy to the darkest depth of agony
And can turn that tide, in an instant,–unprepared –back in an instant–into fantasy

So live each moment, never forget to tell your loved ones, show them–what they mean to you
As in a heartbeat, an event, a moment, a change, will strip you of everything you knew,

And teach you what could possible flitter in the back of your mind,
But needs a lesson–to remember to do everything deeper–, love, live, laugh and be kind
Interesting that I always knew,–I always write and feel life's amazing gift But it never ceases to be a lesson that must be reminded and be a lift,
So that we become the beacon for all those that forget,
And continue to smile and help those that yet,
Have not learned the magical moments in the everyday
And those that continue to bless us, to us, in every way..

Love and laughter always,
Dalia

Our Special Caretaker—Another Angel

There are always special people that walk into your life
More often than not, they come into your home when there is turmoil and strife
This is the story of Andrea, mom's caretaker and now–so much more,
Who would envision that this beautiful lady would care so much and love mom to her core?
It is with so much love in our hearts that we embrace her as well,
As she has watched over Molly, my mom, with such care, and love, how much we can tell,
There are few words as she embraced 4 years gone by after dad died and mom was sad,
She comes every day to chat, to clean, to drive, to laugh and I am so very glad,
That she has come into our lives, and has devoted so much affection and care
To a woman who was a stranger in years gone by, so much has changed
I would not dare
Not doubt Andrea's opinion, her day-to-day understanding of this woman, my mom
I know, beyond certainty, that there is no one more qualified, and keep the calm
When things begin to swirl and mom's needs grow as times often require
Andrea will know what to do and never ever let it become dire
So to this amazing lady, I offer my deepest affection and love
As she is one of mom's most precious angels, a gift from above
It is only for the sake of people like Andrea, such an amazing lady
That I can walk each day with such calm and contentment and no worry,
That my mom's needs are attended to, and with no hurry

SO to my special Andrea, forever grateful for all you are and all you do
Know that you are forever etched in our world and loved every day anew
For without you, mom would not be in such great hands
And for that, forever you are a part of this family, and with no hesitation we can all say that we are your greatest fans

Love and laughter always, Dalia

My special one

It is very rare that you connect with people in a lifetime,
It makes for even more of that special feeling with few in childhood, you find it in your prime,
Even more so, a gift if you can depend on that one to be special at work, you hire,
But this soul, well of course, she waltzed into my life, with energy, and so much fire
She closely resembles my own soul, my own deep sense and core And had no problem not asking but wiggling into my heart,
you can be sure, and now adore
She is special, my Deb who has the light and depth of that born with care
That resembles the love of life as I always chose to feel, to dare,
To offer so much more than most people understand and often are driven
But don't act and allow time and lack of action,
and material things be their 'liven'
But not my Deb, who truly is close to my heart, my soul, my life, my way
With no explanation than love and respect and trust and no matter if far away She will always be a part of me and praying to be closer someday
As I know that her soul is connected to mine, and always she should know

That I will forever know that I am here as whatever she needs,
and my love will grow
As our years ascend and the work becomes less and the friendship more
As I hope she knows she is loved and whatever for
I am here with heart and love in hand
And to that end, I pray I am always in her heart and more than just her friend

Love and laughter always,
Dalia

Marriage Vows

This is the moment, the breathtaking day,
Each moment to be remembered and savored in every conceivable way,
Is it the groom, so handsome in this once in a lifetime role?
Is it the bride so beautiful in her glow as she prepares for that important stroll?

I have no words to express the joy in my heart,
It would take a lifetime to marvel it all from the start,
My beautiful daughter marrying the man she adores,
My one and only precious girl in the love this moment pours,

To the couple, to this moment of magic and elation,
To the depth of your love–never ever lose that sensation,
To thank whatever has brought this fortune to be today,
And to cherish all tomorrows now faced by the two of you, come what may.

To Greg and Nicole, may you always be happy and well,
To a lifetime of promises and infinite stories to tell,
To all those times we will all continue to enjoy and share,
To the hundred of occasions we will have to cherish and care,
For the little girl that stole my heart from the beginning,
And to the man that better work to keep her grinning,

So let me make a toast to this day of joy and splendid grace,
Let the pictures freeze all the happiness in your face,
Let God bless you and yours no matter where you are heading,
Build a wondrous life that captures the beauty of this day, your wedding,
And never ever forget that I am here,
To support, to love, to help, and always, good heavens, be near!

Love and laughter always,
Dalia

Friendship Overseas

I often travel to far away places,
To a myriad of cultures and diverse faces,
And more often than not, I fly and return in haste,
Focused on a mission, and urged not to waste,
Finding no love of the travel or the place I go..
Missing the time home, and the normal routine flow.

So it was with a sense of adventure, of excitement, of Joy,
That accompanied my journey, to explore, to toy..
And so to join my friends, my incredible partners of Energy,
In Ireland, a land of immense beauty and inspiring legendary
And for a few days, to become a tourist, forgetting the Time or the care,
And soaking in the wonders, the scenes, the Cliffs of Mohair!!!

All awhile keeping watch on my friends that frolic And play,
With utmost joy, and not concerned as to what Anyone may say,
And I joined and played and let the energy flow,
We were as young pups, filled with awe and aglow,
Roaming, yet not too hard or too fast,
Stopping everywhere to take pictures, afraid that Something may past…

And in that journey, we met some people, strangers Before,
They welcomed us with open arms, truly special to the Core,
Jimmy and Maureen–how can we ever have know?
That our journey would leave us with such feelings, Since grown?

And blossomed to friendship so true and realistic,
Even more to do with the ease in which it happened, So simplistic..

And so we revere the pictures taken along the way,
Each chock full of its memories, so many each day,
And laughter with pleasure,

At the incredible treasure,
And the place we left, with knowledge we must visit Again,
We are filled with more wonder, and know we will, Just not when,
And so said another, a mystical soul, a prophet who can see,
She chats and looks deeply into the depth of your 'chi'
Bina, her name, living with animals, probably, tame,
And easily blending into this land,
Full of raw enchantment and people so grand.

And so we traveled this wondrous place,
Looking for the Fairies that prance through space,
And finally continued our journeys to complete
And tried hard not to shed the tears that greet
Feelings of sadness and sorrow when saying goodbye
To something so special that instills such a 'high'

And thank you, Dear Lord, for the life and the Pleasure,
The world filled with such wonders, too many to Measure,
And for all the new friends, the strengthening of such Ties,
For that, to all who read, becomes the final testimony
And the reason for our lives.

Love and laughter always,
Dalia

Valentine's Day

So here once more–a year has passed,
I have known you for so long, or is it?–seems that fast
But the 'knowing', the 'you'–that is time and attention required
As we live our lives daily, and often get caught up–busy and tired,
So this special day should allow us to focus on other than work,
Other than the fretting, the hassle, the grind that can lurk,
In each of our lives, in each of our days
And which often leaves us on edge, often in numbness and daze.

So clearly, mein shats,–we have come quite the way
You have become an important part of my life,–magical moments through the fray,
I know I count on your strength and your ever–helpful presence,
I count on knowing I can fall into your arms and soak up the essence,
You will listen, you will gaze, and you will always support,
All I need is a safe haven, and you seem to offer me that forte,

I know you understand many reasons in my hurt and sometimes grieve,
But you also know that I am a warrior, love life and sunshine, yes I believe,
In the best of this life, and what I can do to enhance it, be that hope
And need someone by my side to keep me safe and let me cope
With so much of the strain and stress outside of my soul
And help us live life to the fullest–that is the goal.

So, Happy Valentine's day, mein shats, my darling one,
For all the SOS's, and for all the magical moments and fun,
You and I have much to learn and grow and feel,
I promise to do my best in keeping us happy–that's the deal
I know you need to look inside of you and strike any fears,
As I am not one that will tolerate pity or drama, or long–lasting tears
I want us healthy and strong, in body, in spirit and mind,
As our real lives abound in true love and living well defined

I am enjoying the journey, the love, warmth and desire
I will look to our growth, to the ease as well as the fire,
And the magical moments that are always a part of the plan
Mein shats,–I offer the deepest love–to my very special man..

Love and laughter always,
Dalia

World of Trust

So my charming one, my new found joy and pleasure,
You have given me many magical moments already, happiness beyond measure,
Simple, yet rich, so many feelings to sort, as well as contain
So much to look forward to,–to share, knowing much less pain,
I am indeed inspired to grow always more and more,
The difference, of course is the 'why and what for',

I cannot change the many things I missed, you missed, we missed,
But then again, so much of life, too many phases,–we all 'just exist',
I am already enjoying the many moments, the possibilities,
I am dreaming of all the endless wonders, within our capabilities
I am dreaming of warm touches and quiet days,
And of course, to all the happiness that abounds in life's magical maze.

I am writing to you, my special one–to whom I am giving so much of 'me'
I am curious, and maybe not, for the speed that I share that special intimacy
I know your tender touch and caress,
Your willingness to give me so much happiness–
The natural ease by which you have given me to feel
Leaves me calmer, and happier,–more able to heal.

I look to your many special surprises, and the times we will share,
And the special moments we will explore,,–hmm–if we dare!
This gift to you, this poem, something unique–nowhere to be found,
Except in my heart, and in my mind, and in feelings that abound
I will give so much more than moments of existence and lust
I give this to you, dear sir, with a heart filled with joy and trust

Be well, my charming one,–and do not worry to change the gear,
I am happy, excited, but have promised not to close my heart in fear,
Life is fleeting–so precious, each passing day,

I wish to share it, and love it,–in every way
That is, of course, if you are you ready, if you are easy, if you are 'here'
If you are forever this way, dear heart, I will hold you near.

This, only if you 'let go' your fears and doubts as well
And do not stifle the magic that awaits us, and do not quell
The magic that exists in the moments that we share,
Sometimes fleeting, sometimes too few to bear,
But if you help make this life as it should be–free and light,
Then you have captured my soul,–you will, forever, be my knight.

Love and laughter always,
Dalia

Strange Feelings

My heart is pounding, I pace the floor,
I know what I fear, and yet know, must explore
I yearn for the excitement, and oh, that marvelous touch,
I am in a place I crave so much,
I cannot believe I am losing control
As I already sense it will take its toll,

My body tingles, I am so scared,
My brain says no, my mind feels dared,
I know who you are, and so aware what you feel,
Never ever thought I could be to you 'so close, this real'.

I am so strong, and so very untouchable,
My truth, my integrity, me, so infallible,
I have so much to tell you, this passion only part of the game
Yet, this is not the time, and I must suppress this flame,

I see you so clearly, damn, I feel you to the core,
Of my being, my heart clearly begging for more,
But the ache, it is here, it is what I feel,
It is part of my being I cannot reveal,

Intuition (the 'worm'), you say, yes indeed, it is strong,
That is why I know that I cannot be what I want with you, to belong,
Yet you touched me so very deep,
And awakened something I have long ago, put to sleep

So be proud of your power, my magician man, your manhood, real,
You are in discovery, and finding what you feel,
I will not forget, nor can I, all I can do is sigh,
I have no answers as I search that 'why',

I am too 'rich' in my soul, and too proud to be a passing thought,
But envision what could be, if you were not caught
Forever friends, and yes, to share and, yes, to care,
Remember my smile, and more, if you dare.
In the meantime, I will have to yearn and try to cope,
With the fact that someday,
I may feel this way forever, there is hope
But in the meantime, will relive every touch and feel,
And know that there is a part of me that no one can steal
It is given with all my heart and soul,
To the special man who came in my life to fulfill that role…

Love and laughter always,
Dalia

My Tunte

There was a girl that came to these lands
An immigrant, a stranger to the language and without friends
And even though these times were rough
And always food was scarce and not enough
A love was borne with someone, deep, ever growing
Something special, unbound by blood but ever flowing

With a "Tunte" who cared and chatted and taught
Who smiled and sang and laughed and fought
To keep this girls' mind open and rooted and strong
So that her life and her path could never be wrong
A Tunte who devoted her life and special heart
To a man who had suffered and survived as a part
Of the worst torture dealt any one race
And left wounds to all of us Jews to face

And I smile as I write this to my special Tunte, who
Bought me that book to understand what truly one can do
When challenged by immeasurable odds and no glory
Such courage and gratitude and faith and trust
And a joy for life that is a must
For all of us to practice, from birth to dust

But this poem is not written for sadness or tears
Nor to remember the moments of pain or fears
It is a small gift to one special person I so love
Who has been one of my angels from up above
Who will never be older than thirty-nine,
Who dresses and looks so, so fine

It must bring to you the smile and laughter,
And remind you of 'happiness ever after'

And always, always live and remember
This little girls love that glows with ember
That has intensified as the years have passed
And deepened so as to last
And speared to the ones that now must be brought
To my special Tunte to be taught
Of the wonders of history and language and home
So as to remind us of who we are and not to roam

Love and laughter always,
Dalia

My Adopted Family

It is amazing to be on our journey, as we continue to understand how we evolve our circle of life–
What often seems to be difficult times that breaks your heart and creates such strife,
Yet within the rubble and hurt often left behind in our heart,
There always is a silver lining, new found friends that become such a part,
Of your life, of your important circle,–that grow to such depths of your being,
That they are now family that care, that love, and create such meaning.

That is the story of my Michele and her special family,–now for me deeply imbedded in my heart
Every day I know that I think of them, as they do of me, and forever we shall never truly be apart,
It lets me know that for the very difficult times that were stressful and feelings of gloom
There also was a special bond that was created, like flowers planted and began to bloom,
These amazing moments are not scripted, such feelings may be rare,
All I know is that I have expanded my circle with people I know I love, and I know who care

So in times when I feel that my heart hurts and I think I may feel alone without love
There is a special lady, a family, that have been sent as though from up above, These feelings are as though you are family, as if for certain, we were born to 'be'
It cannot be understood by everyone, most would not dig deep to 'see'
How much love grew from an unexpected event, with such sadness left behind
But the heart does not discern if it was convenient that we were meant to find
Each other and know that our love will continue to grow
And forever you can count on me and mine as those feelings will also flow

To my amazing Michele, Caroline, Mindy and those who I will want, I will adore
I feel so blessed–so surreal to know I am welcome and you will smile when I knock at your door
And the same feelings grow in my heart, as my house is open as open to you always
And my prayers of course that we will find our way to make this happen, counting the days
And I think how lucky to have the opportunity to reach this magical feeling
And know that my circle of live has expanded with more love, while healing

And after all, life is only really about family and friends, at the end of the day
There is nothing more meaningful–and is the one thing no one can take away.

Love and laughter always,
Dalia

My special angel Nadia

There are many people that walk in and out of our lives,
I believe no such incident was an accident, gals or guys
And every one affecting our journey, our paths,
Some who drain us, and hurt our soul–some that bring us joy and laughs,
So as we continue to learn our lessons, hone our goals,
It is often interesting that we encounter people that fill special roles

One such magnificent lady is Nadia, my friend
An angel, no less,–what she brings to my world is additional ways to 'mend'
Not just my body but also my soul and mind,
As it constantly searches for the ultimate purpose of this being to find,
Somehow, I know I am to do much more than I do,
And with Nadia to sooth, and nudge, ah but if you only knew!
Her magical touch, soft voice and direct expression,
Those cannot be replaced as her magic works each session.

So to my most precious lady–my friend
Know that each touch, each morsel of wisdom bestowed, a mend,
Each time I see your face, my world improves in spades,
And the light that you leave,–no–that energy rarely fades,
You are an angel for this lady called Dalia indeed,
And one she appreciates, and always adores –and needs

Be well my Nadia, and never lose touch, as I cherish yours so much
Be well, my special lady, and keep that wonderful smile
As you give me a lift that seems to stay for a very long while,
And as life continues, as our journeys unfold,
And your warmth helps to ease that which could be cold,
You are one of those angels that helps our world glow
And I am grateful as many, to be one special person you know.

Love and laughter always,
Dalia

My Special Extended Family

Nitro

It seems an eternity since you left my world my special soul
Making it very hard to put on paper my feelings,–it has been a goal
For the ones that have passed into our lives (my son's and mine) and made such an impact
Are far and few between, and impossible to write and express without tears–a fact
A fact also that these amazing creatures that surround us each day and night,
Those creatures mean more to us than many humans, as they bring so much light!
My Nitro was beautiful and regal, and a joy every day I had the blessing of his life,
Never ever did he not want my attention and time–and calmed my tumultuous days and strife
He would not care what had been the abundance of problems in the day
All he knew is that I was home and it was time to eat and play
Towards the end it was more eat than play but yet, my attention was what he needed.
And brought such joy to every inch of my body, soul which pleaded
For the break, the peace, the silence of time and the quiet of my brain
So that I could remember the important things, the moments that keep us sane.
I cannot say without breaking my heart and unleashing those tears,
How much I miss him, how much I ache to see those eyes, to stroke away all those fears
Ah–you think it was his fears that I subdued and pretended to ignore?
No–they were mine, as Nitro listened to my feelings, my moods, and knew my core.
Never judging when I rant or raved, had a bad day
But brought me so much joy, so much of himself, his calm, his endless purring
That my world could only be better as I realized better moments are recurring
Only if my attitude makes each day the special day it is meant to be
And that my special boy shared with me many happy feeling–I just need to

be free
Of emotions that held be back, and dark days that have past and should never evoke more pain
And know that he is still with me, forever imprinted in my heart, my soul, my love of life, still my moments of grief I should not sustain
But the monumental amount of love and joy he gave to me and my son, whom ever will continue as those moments that revive the thoughts that bring smiles and will live forever so Nitro–wherever you are wagging that tale as though forever royalty to be served
my special one–will be remembered and loved and a part of me forever, as you deserve.

Love and laughter always,
Dalia

Sammy My special Princess

In the world of cat life, my precious one is very mature, and very wise,
She is the most beautiful creature that I adored from the first time I laid eyes,
On this beautiful girl who started her life in a dumpster, thrown away,
Like garbage, as though she was nothing, so much it hurt to say,
Her belly still carrying the scars of a tattoo created with no regard to her pain,
As she cowered away in the corner, treats and love given in vain,
But I knew she was going to be one special cat, so beautiful, its true
No denying that I knew with some time, she would have a different view
So it came to be that Sammy came home I knew, forever to stay,
With another soul here, thinking it would be natural they would bond, wouldn't they?
Nitro, my first feline, well I thought would be so happy to see,
Another one of his kind, to play, to frolic and enjoy each other and me,
Well those stories of bonding do not always apply to each other it seems
As Sammy made it clear from the start, she was princess, and had her own dreams
Of a house to be pampered–as she instantly changed to be so open–it was stunning
It really strikes hard to know that those creatures destined to die–so numbing
For Sammy represents all those amazing souls that should never be forgotten, and lost
Her soul filled with so much love to give, to save us so we save them at any cost
She came into this house knowing she could know show us her beautiful soul and personality
She walked in with so much attitude her tail–up, she knew she was now family

My Sammy is here every day giving us love and joy, and purrs like the dickens, so loud,
She is still beautiful at 17 as she was the day I brought her in, she is still so proud,
I forever will fight for her and her kind, as she is as special as anything can be
And for the world to know that she is a princess born to grace my life and for all to see.

Love and laughter always, Dalia

Mynka, Our Puppy-Cat

When we first found this girl so feisty, so small, so feral
We had no idea she would grow into our hears and capture it, the heck with any peril.
She ended up being separated from mom, and from the rest of the pack
And found her way into our home, and started opening our hearts just a crack,
It wasn't too long that the love for this girl expanded as she is so precious
And took our hearts and said, 'I am here', my love is infectious

So that is the story of this amazing soul that purrs so loud, it cannot be denied
And demands affection every part of the day and holds you hostage, exuding pride
That she keeps you in her presence, in her warmth and always wants more
Of course, her guardian, her human, my son undeniably spoils her, loves her to the core
It is magical that we have these wonderful souls that come into our life one day
And bless us with so much affection, love and de-stress us in every way
She is forever unforgettable, her huge heart and soul demanding our time and vibe
She is a 'puppy-cat', attached and affectionate beyond words to describe
She is the perfect partner for a couch potato, waiting for food to be fed
And with 'sit' (okay not fetch), has trained 'us', not the other way, as we are now 'led'
But we do it so willingly, so happy to give her all the treats and attention she needs
As it is for 'us' that we do this, fulfilling a place in our hearts that she feeds

Mynka, our wonderful girl, one more special little soul that has stolen our heart,
She is forever making sure her demands her met, and that we are never far apart,

I have hardly ever seen such a bond that so strong, with so much connection
Felines are definitely underestimated for their smarts and their absolute affection
We shake our heads as she continues to amaze us day–by–day
As she pushes the covers from my son's head to feed–she says, 'hey'
Time to pay attention to her, of course, she will not be denied,
The world in our house,–her kingdom and we are forever blessed to be by her side.

Love and laughter always,
Dalia

Bebe
A story of life so fragile

It is so hard to lose something you love so much, so early, and question
The reason, the why, the how, a matter of great strife and reflection,
Bebe came into our lives as a runt, a bubbly, energetic and mischievous little soul,
With a personality so large, so grand, that nothing would help keep her 'in control',
It is to celebrate her life that we write about this special little girl,
And to remember the good times, the moments that have left such a hole
We cannot choose to remember the loss of such a vibrant little bundle of joy
We must choose to remember the reasons she brought fun and was so sneaky and coy
She would take all the clothes out of my drawers and feel it was her place
To totally rip all my clothes and decide it was her space
It is impossible to not giggle when we remember her antics and her look when caught
As to say "well what'? I am here to claim my place, give all the attention she sought
It is still with a heavy heart I write about her dear precious life
But all in all, remembering that we saved her from some very cruel times and strife
She would have been feral and scrounging for food, for water, for warmth and cover
And here, she was our princess, with life simplified, to just frolic and discover
All her special hiding places and yell at us for being late
And always, those funny faces to cheer and smile on our faces to create,
So my precious package of extra spunk and energy and love
We are grateful for all you gave us and hoping you are happy up above
Your memory stays with us every inch of every day
Know your life is remembered and your memories cherished in every way.

Love and laughter always,
Dalia

Sheba
My Special Quirky One

It is difficult to write about this little special soul that I miss so much,
That entered my heart, without question I fell hard, and when she left us early, was crushed,
She was so funny, so different, so quirky so loving in so many ways
I could talk about her antics, so many of them, making us smile for days
So it was heartbreaking to know she was only with us a year,
And how impossible it was to believe that like her sister grieving, it was almost impossible to bear
She was not supposed to 'be' here,–she was a feral, and being fostered,– destined to be given away
But of course, she said, no, I found my home, I think I will just stay
Sheba was mine, in heart and soul, and playful and so close it was special and unique
She did this without permission, and after many months that we concluded she was a bit of a freak
The way she almost sat up to get some sort of a pet, that was so like her to do
And then ran off so you had to come to her–that was her style, hers alone,– that we knew
We have had no choice but to remember all that she gave us, not much time, but oh what a wonder
She was one of the many, but I don't think there was a chance, I could grow more fonder
Of this special girl, that came with antics and with so much love
And now is in our memories, as she frolics and plays from up above
My special Sheba, you came into our lives with little intent to bond, you also were so sick,
It was our job to make you well, but our intent was not for you to stick,
You were to get well and to find a loving home that was someone else's to enjoy
As we know now that was not to be that the story would be ours, maybe that

was her plan, so coy?
As she wormed her way into our hearts, into our daily lives, how could we say no?
As she became so beautiful, so sweet, so quirky in every way, giving us so much joy,
She was a one and only my Sheba, my special one the quirkiest of all who I will cherish for all days
I hope you see us every day knowing that we will never forget you, forever more and always

Love and laughter always,
Dalia

Coco
That special foster failure

There are so many felines that traverse the universe, some fortune, some not,
So it is without question that often Guy and I lend our hand for feral kittens, so many out there but–
We do not intend to 'keep' them–just help them make sure they find a wonderful home,
And give them love and attention and warmth, and remember they are on 'loan'
Well not so for this little soul, that of course, decided she had decided that this was not to be,
Even though the length of time it took her was almost too long, she was not showing us what she could foresee,
No matter how feisty and non–carry her attitude in the early part of her time with us,
She was not going to leave us, she had chosen,
and it was for us to finally understand, regardless of her fuss.
So she has come into our lives, so black we hardly can ever find her even when she is directly in our sight
She has become a part of our lives, showing the affection and love and that cry that depicts her might,
Tiny we thought–but full of 'piss and vinegar' and forever whining so we could serve her little whim,
And us, well we are just her servants, her guardians, but the return of her love and closeness make all that dim,
She is another one of our souls in our lives permanent, as she is close and found our hearts
And all her antics, and all her protests, when she wants something, well that is just her part
To make sure we notice her, she is here and here to stay
And we will need to accept and understand whatever she wants–it is her way
She is a part of the many feral that should be given a chance, and represents

those proudly
As so many of her kind are euthanized every day, in shelters that convince themselves they cannot do more, often cowardly
To work harder to save each and every one, although often it is the community that dictates
Who will live and who will die, as there is not enough recognition of the needs, and seal their fates
But there are many of us that DO care, and do find, and learn that it is education that can save so many more,
And are often blessed by finding these little souls that will forever change OUR lives, will affect us to the core,
That is our Coco, although she came as a pair, and was shy (was she really?) and was reticent to show how much love she will share,
She is now locked so solidly in our being, there is no other like her, and she knows and of course, does not care
She is here, she is loving, she is special, and she is our Coco, another soul who says, try not to love me, if you dare.

Love and laughter always,
Dalia

REFLECTIONS 3

Journey Back
(a Musical)

There are so many of us, as I, that grew up in the dark,
In the shadows; cold and pain leaving its mark;
The world was impossible, Anger, hurt, fear, unstoppable,
How can you see when there is no light?
When all you ever do is cower, broken, darkness and night.

Come on, girl, run for your life into the light!
Let's see what's inside,–that incredible fight!
Fight so the world cannot defeat you!
Might, so that the world cannot beat you!
Fight..to come out of the dark,
This time,,–YOU are the one that is leaving your mark..

Fight..so the world cannot defeat you,
Might..so the world cannot beat you,
Out of the dark.. fighting..leaving your mark

Now, world, MY fight, my might,
And into the light.. as is my right!
And guide others to that destiny,–shining so bright!

Fight, so the world cannot defeat you,
Might, so the world cannot beat you,

Out of the dark, bold, strong;–to always be the light!!

Love and laughter always, Dalia
In the honor of Whitney Houston

Never Getting Old

Our lives hurry by, in a frenzied pace of must's and don'ts and do's,
Of lessons learned and roads to chose,
We all strive to grow, to mature and partake,
Of the sweet nectar of life, whether asleep or awake,

And as we do, our youth flies by,
Our passions outraged, too often we cry,
Too often we wander aimless and lost,
Too often we 'settle' for less, unaware of the cost,

Isn't it strange then, that at any point of time and place,
As so many chapters of our lives have passed in haste,
We look around and realize what we must face,
We reflect and ponder on all that we have done, and why
Why do we do, why didn't we do, so many questions to answer before we die,

Alas, our spirits and souls are the beacons of the heart,
If only we could truly 'listen' to the messages from the start,
Our characters are borne so often straight and true,
Our missions forever launched to find happiness anew,
If only we understood what should be so clear–
Our spirits never grow old….we should never fear!

How can something so beautiful and strong,
How can it be possible that what we do be wrong?
With exuberance and passion, With love in whatever fashion,
We should revel in the sweet gift of life,
And accept that it is always filled with strife,

But the true feelings and powers borne of us within,
Can be unleashed at whatever time we begin,
To unbind our spirits to soar,

Not just in our youth, but forever more,
Embrace every moment, revere in its magic
Not to appreciate it is so sad, so tragic..

Be in awe of the precious moments of every dawn we awake,
It is that, which we do,.. and all that we make,
It is the 'path', the journey of our lives, not the end..
It is our minds, not our bodies, that forever grow and mend..
Forever young, forever growing, forever learning…
Forever curious, forever the desire to understand deeply burning..
Never, then, can this spirit be old..
Never can this burning desire become cold..
The magic inside of our hearts and souls,
The measurement of time never important as our goals,
The wonder of life recreated in an endless odyssey
And God forges our ways and smiles, as he quietly leads the journey…

Love and laughter always,
Dalia

Perspective

What an amazing feeling, this life that flows in our veins,
A kaleidoscope of blood and bone and nerves and brains,
A constant debate that rages between science and religion
That beleaguers mankind, and forever forged in indecision,
Of the larger picture, of the pieces of the puzzle formed from the start
And yet, I alone, as many before and those after me, question,
I, with my heart and soul, log and search constantly for that affection,
That solace, that love, that desire and security we all yearn to find,
In that, I should feel, we are not alone, it is the crux, the mission of mankind,
The need to connect, to find the reason for it all,
The peace of mind that is found once we finally understand our call
Such, then, must be what I will go to sleep and dream and contemplate,
No wiser yet, no closer to what I need to feel is my fate,
I have prayed for help, and I have found answers to many of my 'ills',
Knowing that the angels are busy, and can only accomplish so much for all those, like so many bills,
So on I go, the journey is the greatest joy we have,–that is all there is to know,
Yet it takes us so long, so hard, and maybe never to realize,
that our spirits are borne to grow,
And at the end of that journey, those same spirits are what is left from the ashes to live on and forever glow

Love and laughter always,
Dalia

Reaching for Gold

My life–a paradox of happiness, and strife,
Yes, magical moments and those so painful, they cut like a knife
Deep into my heart, both sides vie for attention,
Deep in my heart, I yearn for peace and magnificent rest,
Deep in my heart, I long for life without pretension,
Etched in my soul, longing, believing,–I will achieve the best.

Yes, I long for love that satisfies both body and soul,
I know I need someone to help me reach my goal,
No, yes,–I can do phenomenal things alone,
But for goodness sakes–why would I?
I wish not to turn my heart to stone,
As I yearn for that magical feeling–why would I lie?

SO yes, indeed,, it is my year to change, to reach,
I must find a way to live those moments, if I could, by the beach,
But whatever I can do to reach deeply into my heart,
I have had enough of times where I may feel forlorn,
There is no reason for me to be far apart,
From those I love, my son, such magic since he was born,
And look to my spirit to help forge my way,
Ah, dear Lord, please send the angels, my fears allay

Deep in my heart,, I yearn for more love, more meaning
Deep in my heart.. I know I am a spirit–gleaning,
Deep, and powerful, my soul is ready to explore
And let my heart skip and frolic, deep to the core.
I was borne to be brave, and reach for the gold,
And I will have it, as the latest chapters of my life unfold.

My thoughts–same as so many aimlessly living
My thoughts, as many in the world, souls breathing,

As their lives progress, and mature and look back,
There is a need, for many, to find ways to give back,
If we have achieved ANY of the things we searched for
Then that gold is that feeling leaving us fulfilled to our core

Love and laughter always,
Dalia

The Future is mine, and to be more

Today is another day traveled, endless time meandering,
I feel no true purpose of soul or passion grabbing my insides, challenging my every cell,
Today is a day I am contemplating, to decide that each day should be much more..more that the travel or the work, or the endless hours of details for it..
Yes, it must be done, and anything done well is dedicated, and focused, and intense, and draining.–that is indeed my work
But inside of me,, a drive too long quelched; a drive to make
a difference, for many not just a few, and empower them as I
feel, with an insatiable drive to live, to love, to give, to embrace,
to respect, to smile and relish in new things, better ones.

So I put forth to myself this poem.. so that I can look at it.. and see the reflection of what I desire so very much. The start of a new project, new direction,,, focus that will create the incredible satisfaction in watching others transform from hurt to better, from empty to fulfilled, from aimlessness to purpose,–no matter what the path and what it has gleaned. Today I put forth my ultimatum.. I wait no more.. I shall investigate my options and carry forth into this next year, a plan to begin opening up volunteer work,,, find the time, the place..no matter.. but start finding other objectives, and decisions renew my life.

So dear God, and the angels that must watch me.
I pray that you will send me on my path and walk with me, and guide my steps, so that I do not waiver, or lose the vision or inspiration that beckons to be heard. Please give me that courage,–and I will forever search for that insatiable goal, and forever I will stay the path I need–I need it for my spirit, who I know I AM,
so that my next years will be a fulfillment of a promise to the high Heavens, and a prayer that you have not forsaken me…

Love and laughter always, Dalia

Thoughts

I am sitting alone at work, my mind such a blur,
Filled with thoughts and emotions, unbound and reckless as they occur,
It is hard to imagine the power and strength I could unleash,
When I learn how to capture and tame them, if I just reach..

And jolt myself into focus, and resolve to do the right thing..
With patience and determination and will to bring
Myself to the pinnacle of my very best, and unbound energy,
A harmonious dance of body and mind in synergy!

Each one of us has the tools, the talent and mind,
To become the ultimate, the most,–each unique one of a kind,
Each has choices, and many paths to journey and partake
It is strange, almost mystical to think of all that we can make.

So I take a deep breath and sigh,
As I realize I have much to journey before I die..
And the strength and energy, so much of which I possess,
Is only now coming to full force, as I master stress..

And my life is blossoming, although turmoil still surrounds,
Every accomplishment finished, a new one confounds,
But my soul more at peace, as I realize what each day holds,
As life is a mixture of many adventures, as destiny unfolds.

Love and laughter always,
Dalia

The flow of life

We are on an endless journey with no true start or true finish,
Being borne to travel to the end, to die, does not diminish,
What is actually a continuation of experiences by which we grow
Of so many lives to bear, yet explore, in an endless spiritual flow..

Thus what paths we chose all have a reason and magical rhyme,
Never to be understood in the dimension or the limitations of time,
It is a sojourn of endless ecstasy and terrible, lonely tragedy,
Manifested in great joy and paradoxical, unthinkable calamity,

Are we lost through this maze, this sea of time and space?
Is there a spiritual state that must be reached,–is that truly the case?
So many questions we could ask, if we stop to ponder,
Yet we explore each day we are on this earth to wander..
And most of us find no solace or magical answers that heal,
Most of the crowd do not find the paths to strengthen or appeal,
To the important part of their spirit and soul,
The reason for living and what often takes its toll,

Questions, questions.. does it really matter what it could mean?
When you look around, what is left, what can we glean?
Some of us trek on an endless journey to nowhere,
Those people seemingly live without a doubt or care,
Others spend all their time searching for what, or..why
In reverence of something, lost or found,.. oh my, oh my…

In truth and in honesty, in blatant disregard of the fears,
Life has no meaning if we cannot love so deep as to bring us to tears,
Whether it be someone, or something, a friend, lover or object,
Whether it be physical, mental or spiritual manifestation as the subject,
It must be deep, it must be true..
Colors of the rainbow in all their glory and hue…

So passes our lives,, the time ticks away,
We endure hardships and pain, only to realize the way..
For if we are to truly understand the depth of our feeling,
We must have learned to understand the intensity of the healing,
That comes with empathy and compassion and care,
Forever to repeat in endless lessons that started in despair..

But those that endure and heal and grow,
For those that understand the world, and God's ebb and flow,
The reward is the richening of everything that is important to feel,
Inexplicable and illumines,–unique with the intensity of something so real.
Sad, isn't it.. that we must suffer to understand what is life..
What is beautiful, what is important begins with so much strife.

Listen! ..Listen, I say.. as I say this with all my hearth..
Do not search outside, do not become lost, or try to finish from the start.
Our lives are meant to be filled with so many tests of who we are..
We must trust ourselves, and the voice inside never far..
And enjoy each day.. experience as children in God's paradise…
Enjoy each pain and blessing alike.. take my advise..

Sojourn in peace.. and in simplicity and deep emotion
Forever your way, your travels with love and devotion..
And the road light and filled with incredible sensation
And that all that we are and will be–parts of creation..

Love and laughter always,
Dalia

Who Inspires me?

I am in an extraordinary spot in time and place,
Decisions, and deeds, and life to face,
I know I have loved ones that will not bear to lose my heart,
And my heart–it tells me how much all of you are so much a part,
And yet, I search, as most of us do,
For more, for many, for fulfillment, for peace, for love,
Yet it is so hard to reach and that ultimate connection, finally, from above,

But we connect down here, with a few angels, aren't they?
One of them lives too far away, although a part of me each day
Yes, every one of us entering my life, are so much a part of me,
That it is hard to pass each day without a vision I see,
Of many that have touched me, and times shared in laughter and song
And things that could not possibly ever go wrong..

All of you special–you must be well, I cannot live alone,
You are a part of me. no matter distance, no matter how much we moan..
You must stay well, as I count on all of your presence, my armor and shield
I am that, indeed, but alone, impossible,–but with all of you, invincible,
I will not yield,
My life determined, my path still straight and aware of what I must do
That I can make a difference, forever more, I will ascend to heights so true.

And, my friends, my family, a part of that magic, my most cherished,
As all of you are as a part of me, saving me as a soul that almost perished,
And brought me life, and knowledge that the world could be more,
The world depends on us, those that must make us better in the core,
As it will take so much energy and immense spirit to fulfill,
Yet.. it must be–as our lives are given–we have free will.
So take heed my special ones,,
You must stay well,, you must teach my son…

That life is fleeting..only a few magic moments to sustain,
But we have many incredible feats to attain,
And the energy, the joy, the hardship, the love, the connection
Comes from those that hold us and keep us–and all of you that care,
No words for how much I love all of you, the affections,
Forever lives the heart, the soul, forever,
The images of your presence today,–and always your reflections.

Love and laughter always,
Dalia

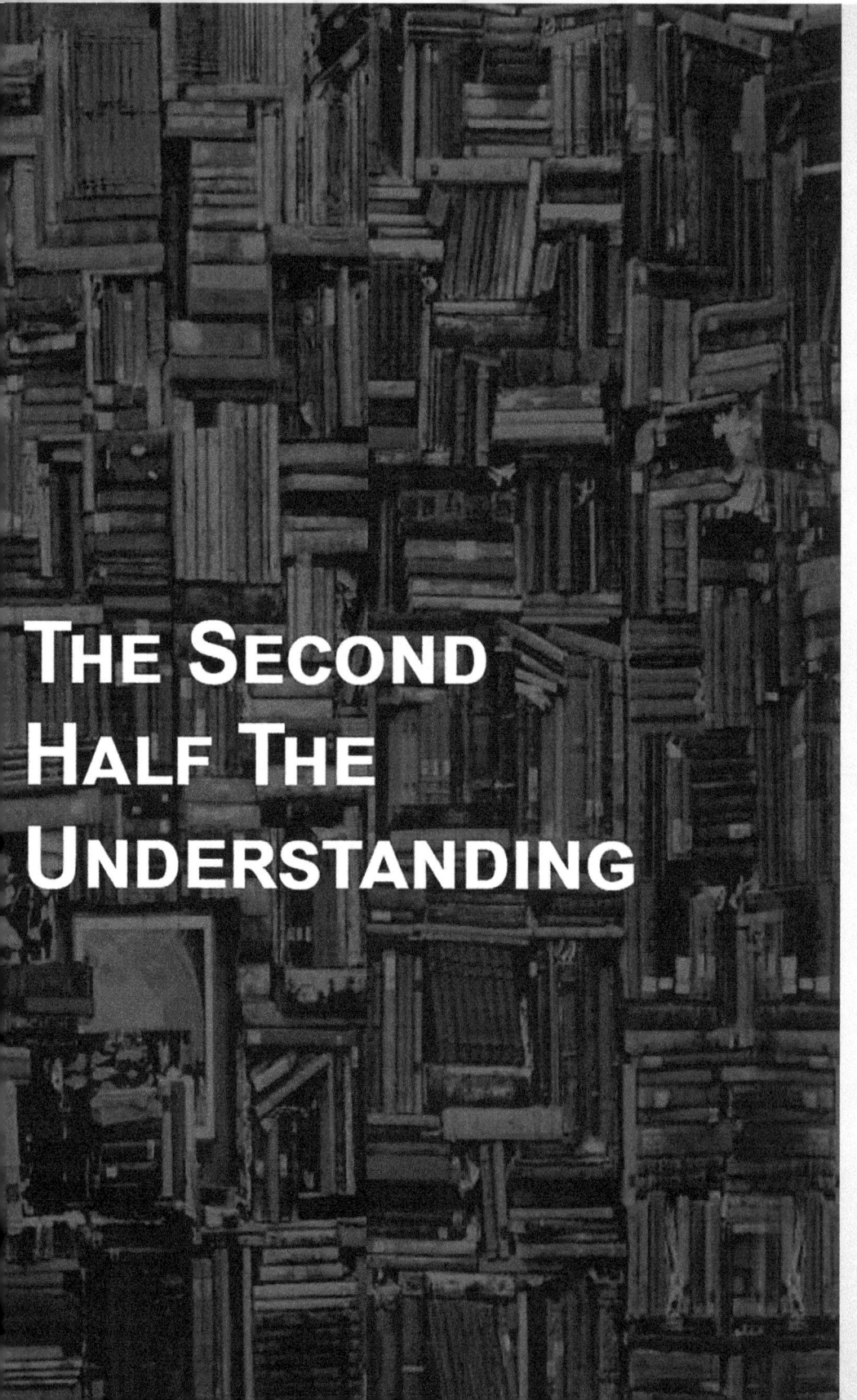

The Second Half The Understanding

Reflections 3

How, dear Lord, can I do what is right,–what will help teach my destiny?
How do I walk through the maze, and define what seems an eternal mystery?
I feel that I must do so,–I must have the answers,
I am tired that I do not, I must have learned what
I need to know–why do I feel I cannot?
I have so much control, yet sometimes so little,
I have so much to do, yet often it seems my life is one big riddle.

On another passing of another year and all it is meant to be
I can count the important blessings of my life, as often we fail to see,
It is not the things we want, and what we do not have,–as we easily forget,
It is all that we have, that we passively cherish, and yet,,
We look to the Great one, the Divine, to guide our steps, our way,
Hoping and praying that if we believe, if we look to him, he will save the day…

No,, no,, that is so wrong,–that is not how it is supposed to be..,
We are the ones with all the strength inside, we must believe in ourselves, in what we foresee,
We are the ones that can change the world, not the faith that is God's to teach
Because it is God that has taught us to be what our destiny must reach,
And become all that we think we can be, if we really believe,
And dream all the wonders that our minds and souls can conceive.

And dig deep Within our hearts, our souls if we must,
And think of what we do every minute of birth to dust,
We should leave a mark, not in the sand to be washed away,
It should be etched into the memories of the new generations that will say–
These people made our future a better place,
Each one offered their very best, and this world to grace

Love and laughter always,
Dalia

Contentment

And so I sojourn to another state, another day passing by
Not really feeling fulfilled as yet, something to feel before I die,
No–not at all do I feel trapped or not happy with my life
I feel blessed more than ever, even as it seems I am full of strife
I have so much gratitude, so much to say thank you
to the spirit and angels above
I breathe deeply, contemplating that I am healthy, and that I do have so much love,

I have a wonderful son who loves me, and I cherish him so much,
To be blessed with such a child, everyone should feel that touch,
As many times we do all we can and fail to end with such a good soul
And we often end our lives embittered, in a hope–the child's goal,
And so much of me feels strong, yet I yearn to have more, do more
Is that wrong? Is there nothing short of pure happiness deep to our core?

I am constantly questioning my own wisdom or lack of it in life's fray
But I also know that I 'see' more than many the magic of each special day
I am never satisfied with my own limitations, my own self–doubt and churn
As I also know that my soul is limitless and the energy inside me continues
to burn
So dear lord and the angels above
I will continue this journey and know that each day
I am learning to love Life and the love of myself which has been the hardest
thing to feel
As I also know that I will sojourn with intentions and with the mind that
says that I am special, as are each of us are and that feeling, so surreal

This poem is meant to bring forth and inspire,
To raise the level of passion that is within us–that fire..
It should be the mirror to look inside and see,

There is no one without it,
Whether you or me…
The trick,–the magic–is the question of time,
For those that care find the reason and rhyme,
And become the 'masters' of their hearts and soul.
As has been, and always will be the goal.
And then will lead all the others that arise
And help guide the tiger in his quest to be wise,
As the dragon's force is strong but tame,
Although it's energy boundless, and always aflame.
And those that follow the true sense of this world,
Are the best of mankind, the wise and the bold.

Strive to be one or the other in your hear,
For each has the power, and the spiritual part,
To bring you to new heights, new experiences, new life,
And open the door to those possessed only with strife,
And become the special, the gifted, the leaders to be
With the courage, the vision, the dragons and tigers for all to see

Love and laughter always,
Dalia

Who You Are

I have always been unusual in all I do and the intensity of how I live,
I have always had around me those I love and to whom I give,
But even harder to find and harder to keep is someone as deep as you,
To share the moments I laughed and cried and always somehow knew
That I needed a shoulder, a friend to share, whatever whims may bring,
Someone who cares for me, and shares whatever songs I want to sing.

I cannot truly do justice to what I feel, so hard to express,
For your love, your support, your presence through all the times, and all the stress,
I have also inflicted the pain whether I will 'fess' to it or not,
For the truest love of all is the one you show, the one no matter what,
The one that is always there, that I can count on at any time of day or night,
What can be given more to bolster someone with such strength, such might?

I will only say, my dearest one, that there is also that love back, so deep, so true,
Wherever you are, whatever will be,–it sparkles as though lit anew..
You have only to ask, not even that.. just say,
That you need my support, my friendship–I'll find a way..
To make you know that I am as true to you as you are to me..
That what I feel is not given to many, but for only a few to see…

We will continue our paths, and hopefully banter along the way,
And talk and see the wonders of our world, each day, and play,
That is the ultimate of what we should know as we wake anew,
That we are our own masters, our destinies forged by what we think and do..
And so, keep forging ahead, with the help of those spirits, like you so rare..
Remember that you are my blessing, and I, my self to you, like the sun's shining Glare.

Love and laughter always,
Dalia

A Special Day

There are many people that we meet day to day
We often do not understand how they matter, in what way,
Some that we care for, or vice versa, though world's apart
Some that will leave an imprint, forever in our heart,
Some that will pass right by us, and never know,
And some that will stay, and our feelings forever grow

Some very spiritual, searching for ways to improve our souls
Knowing that we mere mortals think it can be done as goals,
But truly, it is a matter of journey, and faith, and what is inside,
And individual feelings, and needs and desires,–that guide our light
It is hard to believe that we can make a difference to this world,
But there are many of us, dedicated, caring and bold

Thus, my point–you are one of those that does dare,
That shows your faith, your dedication, and care,
I know I am in good hands, with loyalty and devotion on my side,
As you are not the typical, not the norm,–and one I can confide,
All my issues, and concerns,–my worries and fears
And brings calm to my world, in finance as well as my tears

So dear sir, I know you will continue on your journey, your path,
You will do so, as an example of love, of gracious hope, not wrath,
You will always 'be' there when things grow dark,
And will offer that faith, that hope, that eternal spark,
So please, enjoy this special day, and all those as you grow
And remember someone is always a fan, as you well know

Love and laughter always,
Dalia

Emerging anew

It is the year 2000, can you truly fathom that we are here?
Living into the next century, into the time anticipated with such fear?
A time full of challenge, full of wonder and events, sometimes strange
A time of technology the likes of which we never knew,–signs of change,
Change in our attitude, in our view of ourselves and the world,
A time to reflect but take action, and leap, or be hurled.

For this next generations will not be led or wait,
They have seen what was there, and will not let it be fate.
They have watched the destruction, of ourselves and our planet,
They have witnessed the disgrace of our wars, and faces of granite,
The tormented souls surviving atrocities and hatred,
And the diminishing populace of creatures we should hold sacred.

It is the dawning of a new time, a new race,
Of mankind, with a stronger mind and gentler face..
Of those that care about each other and the environment to torn,
That we must protect every bit of it, and all the ways to learn,

To protect what is left of the beauty that surrounds mankind,
And learn to share all that we have with rich the poor, the blessed the blind,
Is this not real, is it a dream that only the idealist babble throughout the days?
Is it not possible that the dawning of the century can lead to wise and
gentler ways?

Of course, and as it should be–it must
We have learned the lessons of youth, and have grown to trust,
That, just as children whose lives grow with exploration and mistakes,
The purpose to such is to evolve and understand the seriousness of the stakes,
And revel in sharing the abundance and serenity some of us have found,
And scatter it around the world, so that the magic of happiness will abound!

Why not you ask? Why cannot this be done?
For each passing day is symbolic of the renewed glow of the sun,
Each new beginning a testimony that we have mastered our demons and remnants of any dark deed,
That our energies are restored and ready for the journeys ahead and our will to lead,
Each new life that is born can be instilled with drive to succeed,
In making this world a better place, and to all others, to heed,

That there is no tolerance for living in hatred or sin,
The world has had enough, we are better that what we have been,
We are nations brought together to be unified, not torn,
We can create a planet of joy, for all those yet unborn,
Our children, our destinies, our eternity looming bright as the century continues to unfold
And bring forth the light that will guide us through glorious stories, yet untold.

Love and laughter always,
Dalia

Moments of Time

I continue to explore the world around me as I navigate this life,
I have often intensified, often doubted,
often wished that I had fewer lessens that have cut my soul like a knife.
I love life and believe I have an open and willing heart,
Reality though tells me that those feelings are so ambivalent and often my own self is torn apart.
Not rational, and not full of drama or obvious to most of those that surround me,
I often exude a life of intense passion and love which are true, but definitely not care–free
I wish to find the love to share with someone
I feel deeply for, And can give of myself everything I have to the core,
That is definitely something I covet and wish to achieve,
Although it seems elusive and harder and harder in which to believe

So I will continue to focus on the things I love and deeply care,
My work, my passion to help those that have no voices and where I dare
To make a huge difference as these matters often seem irrelevant and small,
To those I can help I am definitely a hero that stands rather tall
I cannot say why this journey is taking so long, so many twists and turns
But indeed my blessings are many, and so many 'learns'
I will continue to be the me, the deeply committed one I know
And will send out to the high heavens my gratitude
as the best of me continues to flow
And forever continue to build my eternal soul, the best of me
As I find that most people look at the world but cannot 'see'
The importance of love and the care of those souls that do need our protection
And offer those around me and the innocent ones that deserve my love and affection

Love and laughter always,
Dalia

Today

There is the birth like the sunrise of every day we live,
And then, there is the end, like dusk of that same day, I believe
Precious moments, so many, so rich and bright,
They are like sprinkles of magic for us to savor and delight!

What a strange thought, you read and wonder!
I must be seeing this day in a different world, you ponder!
Not every day that we live is beautiful and true,
There are days when we are so melancholy and blue!

No, my friend, it is not so by design…
The life we have is very, very divine.
It is our own minds, alas, that we must refine,
That work to interpret the days as our thoughts define…

Yet, the worst of our experiences cannot suppress,
The beauty around us and those touches that caress,
We have only to capture the sight, not only to see,
We have only to energize from the touch, not only to be…
Today is no longer–, leaving only the slightest of imprints behind,
Tomorrow will be borne,–take a moment and so remind,
Yourself and all others of the joy and sweet taste,
And be grateful for the precious moments,–do not haste.

We are what we chose, through that world in our mind,
We can fret and worry and be angry, not kind,
But at the end of the birth and death of our wondrous days,
All that will matter will be the spirit that stays,
Ever more rich and ever so much stronger,
Grateful for all it had experienced and yearning no longer…

Love and laughter always, Dalia

A Day in the Life

We awake to the hustle and bustle of what we do
For the baker, the bread baking in the dusk and the dew,
The farmer milking the cow and feeding the herd,
Going about his business, not uttering a word..
Mothers rouse to feed their young and appease their cries,
While the rest of the world slowly stretches to rise.

Am I talking about the life so hectic today,
Buzzing around with beepers, E-mails, faxes that can't delay?
Our lives have taken on a different kind of hew,
Our waking hours demanding, and lighthearted moments so few,
Our loved ones and friends connected by E-mail
And the fiber of our relationships threaded so frail.

Our pace so dizzying, our thoughts so frazzled,
We spin and turn, feeling frantic and dazzled,
With so much to do while the clocks tick and chime
Stop the dizzying pace, arrest that time!

Take a good hard look–breathe deep..
Slow those inner thoughts and each one keep..
Precious and bright… feel alert and strong
Each moment created, each thing you do, never wrong
Experiences to enjoy, to savor and love
Soak in the world, feel the dirt to your feet and the wind above.

For each person toils and labors with care
Each of us lost in work but each with a story to share
Whether the city's bright lights and crazy pace
Or the calm, but hard country life is what you face
Such are the choices we all must make,
Revel in the magic as each day emerges and we awake.

The farmer keeps pace as his cows meander on the trail…
The babies now sleeping, looking so sweet and frail…
The cities morning haze sweeps over thousands in the street,
All busy and anxious as to what work will greet…
This is our life as we awake each day
Our work fills our moments, our minds far away
We look towards the stars, sigh and mystically dream
Time to throw away that phone & beeper, and relax by the stream!
Forget the computers, take up the paint and the brush
Listen very carefully, there is such a wondrous story in the hush!
Change your clothes from suites to simple wear
Feel the reward of your spirit rising and your soul abound with care!

Love and laughter always,
Dalia

Moments of Time

I continue to explore the world around me as I navigate this life,
I have often intensified, often doubted, often wished that I had fewer lessens
that have cut my soul like a knife.
I love life and believe I have an open and willing heart,
Reality though tells me that those feelings are so ambivalent and often my
own self is torn apart.
Not rational, and not full of drama or obvious to most of those that
surround me,
I often exude a life of intense passion and love which are true, but definitely
not care-free
I wish to find the love to share with someone I feel deeply for,
And can give of myself everything I have to the core,
That is definitely something I covet and wish to achieve,
Although it seems elusive and harder and harder in which to believe

So I will continue to focus on the things I love and deeply care,
My work, my passion to help those that have no voices and where I dare
To make a huge difference as these matters often seem irrelevant and small,
To those I can help I am definitely a hero that stands rather tall
I cannot say why this journey is taking so long, so many twists and turns
But indeed my blessings are many, and so many 'learns'

I will continue to be the me, the deeply committed one I know
And will send out to the high heavens my gratitude
as the best of me continues to flow
And forever continue to build my eternal soul, the best of me
As I find that most people look at the world but cannot 'see'
The importance of love and the care of those souls that do need our protection
And offer those around me and the innocent ones that deserve my love and affection

Love and laughter always,
Dalia

My wish

What would be my wish for the world today?
What would you want to your children to say?
What is it that the holidays express, or do they?
What have we lost, to regain if we are to improve our way?
All these questions in times of turmoil and disarray,
Simple answers, indeed, needed to calm the fray.

How? So simple, we often lose sight of our needs,
They are a matter of abundant and often good deeds,
Not expressed with money or huge time to take
But a few simple moments, not hard to make,
Little deeds of humble affection,
Can wipe out years of hurt and rejection.

Passover and Easter–remembrance of an important day,
Packaged with family and friends, and time to pray,
What I would wish for all to know,
What needs to be expressed, what words to flow?

Oh, so easy, so light that we often forget its might…
Need it be words, or a smile so bright?
Often in silence, the victory is ours,
A laughing face, a hug has such incredible powers, My wish?
Oh yes–that the holiday be our guide,
To bring all that we lost back, set aside the pride,
Bring back the look, the touch, the feel,
Let all of us rejoice, and thus, begin to magically heal.

Love and laughter always,
Dalia

Perspective

What an amazing feeling, this life that flows in our veins,
A kaleidoscope of blood and bone and nerves and brains,
A constant debate that rages between science and religion,
That beleaguers mankind, and forever forged in indecision,
Thus I sit and ponder how my significance can be such a part,
Of the larger picture, of the pieces of the puzzle formed from the start.

And yet, I alone, as many before and those after me, question,
I, with my heart and soul, long and search constantly for that affection,
That solace, tat love, that desire and security we all search to find,
In that, I should feel, we are not alone, it is the crux, the mission of Mankind,
The need to connect, to find the reason for it all,
The peace of mind that is found once we finally understand our call.

Such, then, must be what I will go to sleep and dream and contemplate,
No wiser yet, no closer to what I need to feel is my fate,
I have prayed for help, and I have found answers to many of my ills,
Knowing that the angels are busy, and can only accomplish so much for all those, like so many bills,

So on I go, the journey is the greatest joy we have,–that is all there is to know,
Yet is takes us so long, so hard, and maybe never to realize, that our Spirits are borne to grow,

And at the end of that journey, those same spirits are what is left from
The ashes to live on and forever glow…

Love and laughter always,
Dalia

Change of Course

So it is meant to be, my path to whatever I claim,
Not sure what it means in life's inevitable game,
My passion for life, my will to be a success,
It is certainly never easy, that I will definitely profess..
I have changed my course, my work and my home,
For a world of new wonders, new places to roam.

Life is an endless flow of time and space,
There is no need to rush, it is not a race
Where we go,–never seems to be what 'they' say
Why we go, never to be understood, at least not today,
When we go, always looms as a question of luck and time,
How it happens seemingly little reason or rhyme.

So whatever road our destinies lead to be,
The things to remember should be the obvious to see,
Be aware of what we have, regardless of our choices,
The simplest of pleasures, the reasons our heart rejoices,
The beauty of each and every precious day
The time to absorb the world,–not its fray.

Go out, enjoy–go play…
Do the things you wanted to do,–without delay.
No matter what path, what course, what direction,
Make sure it is filled with tons of affection.
And share it,–and today–, with people you meet every day,
That is what is missing, the link to life's golden ray.

Love and laughter always,
Dalia

Our Paths Unfold

Our lives are a journey, in constant motion and pace,
The world we know, forever in constant ebb and flows we face,
For all of us who search, and all who seek,
For all that aspire to be more than the meek,
For this world is not for those that cannot be bold,
As our spirits learn through time, as our lives unfold,
We cannot be less than what was intended,
Our spirits search, and hunger for what is splendid,

The 'me' the 'us' that cannot be denied,
And often we suffer when that search is defied,
We must, we need to find our way,
Our paths determined through strife and what may,
Ah, that is the lesson,–the journey itself,–our 'heart'
We look and we search, and we seem worlds apart,
And wonder why we cannot find that peace in our souls,
As we find ourselves, if ever, as the embers of our own coals,

We, alone, are that lights that shines inside
Those incredible spirits that are our constant guide
So everyone one of you, and everyone one of me,
Reach to ultimately overcome all, and be,
That magical something that our journeys intend,
To reach that remarkable depth only felt beyond 'pretend'

A feeling achieved only once this is found,
Ah, at last, you understand, as you may discover the 'you',–that can astound
But always, please always, never take for granted, each moment, each breath
For living each day is the magic, the secret, what truly separates us from 'death'!

Love and laughter always,
Dalia

My Life

I reflect on all the days gone by,
My heart aflame with emotions that question why–
I am desperate to do so much more than I do..
A privilege reserved for the very few–
That have figured out that life is not to be denied,
That we all lived whether we laughed or cried.

And that passion should flow or we just survive
And miss all the wonders that make us feel alive.
God grant me the power to do the things I need to do..
And grow and learn and love anew.
As time will heal all my wounds and mistakes
And melt them away like so many snowflakes
And be that special inspiration to all that need to know
That yes indeed, one can pass the pain, and grow

Yes, indeed,–we all have to live our lives and understand
That heaven can only be found when our spirits land
In that special place of peace and serenity
Only received and accepted with the flow of our good energy!!
So go out and live that life you are meant to live
And know that you are also bound to the laws to give
All that you have in spirit and nothing matters except that soul
The one that will create and live, or there will be a toll
Love yourself and everyone around you–do not cower
To be found only once you understand yourself, the true Power

Love and laughter always,
Dalia

My Journey

My journey continues, my path winding, ever flowing
My spirit always searching, yet my light every glowing,
What drives us to live the lives we do–?
What defines who we are–me and you?
How does our character grow and expand,
When we are so different and many, like pebbles of sand.

It may be a puzzle never to be solved,
Like so many challenges, always begging to be resolved.
But all there is–is the process of life,
To be enjoyed and cherished, in joy and strife!
At the end of our journey–we all find the same–
It is how we journey that defines what we are in name,
It is our courage, our will, our strength, our flame,
Always the highroad, integrity, never in shame..

For at the end, in the flicker of time called living,
Our souls are defined by the act of giving,
The more we are open to goodness and love..
The easier the path that leads from above..
Go forth–the many, the brave and the strong..
That are grateful and know they belong,
A part of God's pride of creation,
And the eternal, immortal part of our foundation..

Love and laughter always,
Dalia

Serenity

The word so easy, so simple, so true It helps ease us, when we feel so blue,
Funny, I believe, in mayhem and turmoil our world churns each day,
So few of us comprehend that we need to find some peace to ease the way,
Is it with someone to hold, someone to love, a passion that must be found?
Is it with dealing with life's many mysteries that have few answers,–
confound?

I know we search for that simple truth, that 'place' so special, that inner joy,
I also know today, that life cannot be explained, that we live to experience,
to toy,
We cannot change what we cannot control, although our life is ours to forge,
We say 'no choice', when we chose not to honor, but to 'gorge'.
And often more than not, the essence of life slips by,
And the youth, the passion, the story that instilled our vision, will so easily
let die.

So back to the story, the place we said we want to be,
That magical place we say captures hope and joy, called serenity,
In every thing that I seek, to embrace the passion, to fight without tire
In every aspect of my life, my choice, my desire, my fire,
I also know that it must be tempered, it must have a balance, and some
peace I must have solace, and a quiet spot, where life's hectic style must cease

And in that vision of immense quiet and joy, of an inner view,
I imagine that these poems will flow, will come easier, with some, much
brighter hew,
Yes, because I can paint so much deeper, the thoughts in my mind,
Enriched with the solace, and peace of a place I finally find,
Rich with warmth, with endless dreams and visions that are good,
Instead of the nightmares that haunt me, allayed with the calm that can help
seclude,

So bring on Serenity, that calm that inner state, that is ours, and mine, a quest
I am near, I am close, I can feel that this life, always a challenge, is no longer a test,
I know I can journey, embrace, still explore, and so desire, the next phase,
Clear as my senses are sharpened,–my Self less confused,–the journey less the maze,
Ready to embrace Serenity into my heart, as it is not abstract or unreal,
It is indeed a part of my strength, and something to share, as I wish,–as I chose to feel.

To all you who wander endlessly through life' many emotional chapters
Remember that only we, the I, the You, can commit to finding the calm and the laughter
And when we do, the sun shines brighter, and the magic reappears
No matter the insanity surrounding us, the cold, the hunger, the fears
Yes–quite an eternal optimist with visions to bring serenity to the world,
In many forms, in many ways–and a trend that for many has yet to unfold..

Love and laughter always,
Dalia

My eternal optimism

So my journey continues in a windy path, not clear as I would hope
And my heart still gray, not sure of how to cope
And continue to look for my angels who can help set me straight
As I traverse the world, with work I pray will be a path to my fate
I yearn for the days I can share my life, my libido, my mate,
And so that journey continues with its many twists and turns
And my life evolves with the hope that I may finally succeed through the fire in my heart that so powerfully burns
That fire that leads me to desire to do good, to find a way
To make this world somehow a better place to stay
So I am in continuous mode to try to improve the world
And be strong, always looking for my plan to unfold
To bring my goodness to those who need,
Whether in the physical, or in a spiritual need.
So to my world, to my friends, to all those that love me,
I know I will make something powerful yet, to be
That special spirit you endowed my mind to hold
And to bring that type of change from a world often cold
And to enlighten, and bring warmth and inspire
To all those who surround me, who know I cannot tire
As I traverse the world, and find my way
I will always believe that I can truly be that special ray
Of hope, of inspiration, of all that I can be
And all that I was meant, and all that is me
I know I can do more, and I will, I promise today
So that there are no regrets, and so strongly I must pray
Today my angels,–listen to my heart and my soul
Guide me–help me, to achieve my goal
Mankind to be better, my life to be shared
And all those that surround me, will be cared..

Love and laughter always, Dalia

World of Possibilities

Endless worries, endless frets,
That is often our lives–many debts
We live, yet not, as our lives unfold,
So many stories as we search–so much pain untold
We crave for what we cannot find,
The weight of today, the price for this incredible mind

All our journeys end with the same finality, our death.
Our lives nothing–but our legacy, not about our breath,
We have endless ways to move the world, while we are here,
Yet so much energy is devoted to things we fear,
Our work, the daily grind, the hassle, our need to sustain,
We constantly succumb to our needs, our pain,

Life is so rich, so much about love and devotion,
So much heart in our friends, family–that emotion,
Nothing nurtures our being more,
Nothing can replace what must be replenished in our core,
The possibilities are endless, if we just can let go, and 'be', The journey amazing, if our love flows free
Ah yes,, life–what a wonderful journey beyond our wildest dreams
If we can breathe with abandon, with love that beams
A possibility–a goal, for all that live day by day
Yes–to live, to 'be', not just exist, beyond the fray
Live as though life ends today,–death is near,
And that magic, our meaning, will overcome our internal fear.

Love and laughter always,
Dalia

Dalia's Strong Self Emerges
The New Chapter

Life without meaning, without passion, without reason is not life
To follow the path with the wisdom learned, hard fought in strife,
That is how these chapters evolve, that is how your spirit morphs,
Or you break through the tears, the years, the pain that dwarfs,
And become that which is buried deep inside, waiting for the sense to awaken
For yourself, for your strength, for your soul cannot be taken

I am in awe of life and the hurt and destruction mankind can create
But I believe in a higher power; nothing, no one meets if it isn't fate
I have traveled many highways and by-ways as most of us must do,
It takes a special breed to persevere, the tough, the determined, the few
It takes a strong will, an unwavering passion, to tear the shackles that hold us back
It will take a life-time for the strong to recognize that we cannot crack
I am on a new path today, given strength by a special breed of who we are,
That can only happen with some power, some magic, inexplicable by far.
Whom am I then, who has risen from the hurt and the scars,
Whom do I say lives and breathes in her new form and eyeing the stars
As I cannot hold back what has finally been unleashed

Watch out world, Dalia is here, and ready to be reached
Watch out my cherished friends and those yet to be
I am following my heart to better times and places
And ready to also meet destiny with new journeys, and new faces
And carve out a place that will help improve whatever I can
With the experience and wisdom in my special plan
And continue to grow and immerse myself to it all
The destiny born of everything I finally understand in my soul, is my 'call'

Love and laughter always,
Dalia

Time to Write

It is time to write as I enter this New Year,
It is time to write my desire to meet life head on,–leave behind my fear
I am ready, I do believe, for the life yet ahead,
I am so full of anticipation, of this chapter to be read
I look to the heavens,–and to my core as well,
As I know that I have journeyed long,–of course, that is impossible on me to tell!

My life rich with experience, so good and so bad,
I have once yearned for death, unimaginable,–and sad,
That I,–that someone, could reach lows so low to make that call,
And so out of control, that it was easier to fall,
Prey to the worst, and to the thought of such madness
Prey to our mind's own fears, our own sadness,

But here I am, amazingly mighty and strong
Here I am–the gal that survived, with so much more right than wrong
Here I am writing the world of my will, of my power
Here I am as tall as I can tower,
As I proudly move forward to etch these words into your heart,
I am certain that so many of us are all a part,
Of a higher energy, a power to explore and thrill
I am living life with joy, and wonder–and free will.

Next steps–watch out.. as this lady continues to evolve
Watch out, world,–as I deepen my resolve
To make this world a better place,
And find a way to brighten someone's face
As many as possible, as far as I can reach
Happiness and joy and smiles–that, and more, I will teach…

Love and laughter always,
Dalia

Time is Passing—Emotions strong, lasting

I am so amazed by the length of time we have shared this year–mein shats and more
I often think of all the busy times in my life–and wonder 'what for;
You are there to help keep my spirit remember how much life I adore

All in all–to share one's life–and not be alone or sad,–enriching in many ways,
That is what is important as life's ebb and flows pass in so many days–

But to know that there are those that care so much, as I see in your gaze
I hardly can imagine my luck, and comfort for one so tender and so amaze
My life is indeed so much easier when you are here and near,
But still tire of fighting those dragons,–often have a heart left full of fear,
Life is beautiful, sensual, amazing,–so much to be seen and touched,
I am yearning for every minute to be adored, to be enhanced,–not to be rushed.
And so much more of this life, to be shared, to be explored–not alone
You have given me many magical moments and days,–
and affection when I tire to the bone,
Mein Shats, you have given me so much strength, and so much of yourself,
I love our times, and look to empower us even more
Sharing is easy for me–trust a great deal harder, as I hurt to the core
But nothing that should prevent our magic–and bond
from the wonders that await with 'more'
I am here, and always, in the many moment to enjoy the depth of life each day

As I continue my journey to someplace good, and did indeed acted upon a dare, but cannot suffice,
I am still dreaming of possibilities that this could go on forever,
But as my brain will eventually conquer what is so magical, but probably not clever,
It is knowing that I am not in the right age, the right time, the right circumstance,
I cannot even tell the world, to shout the love aloud, to twirl and dance

But goodness, it is a such a gift–that is all I can hope to have for as much time,
I am in my prime, and he, still children to raise,–not exactly in rhyme
But when we are together, even apart–
Our feelings are so huge, so heart–to–heart
When we are together, our every bit is in so much harmony
A glorious feeling that is in so much magic, it must, it must, be destiny.

Okay.. I will hang on for this unimaginably amazing feeling
As I cannot fight when I know I will lose when I see him and he has me reeling
And I will fall into his arms, his kisses engulf me
Open my core, my being, the me that so few ever see
And I will surrender to its immensity,–not fight–
I cannot imagine that this cannot be right–
And leave myself to whatever destiny this is meant to be
I know that this will, this must–bring me to someplace–and to harmony

Love and laughter always,
Dalia

Love and Laughter always

www.ingramcontent.com/pod-product-compliance
Lightning Source LLC
Chambersburg PA
CBHW051502080125
20076CB00054B/914